HERSTORY
Reveals His Glory

Copyright © 2015
M. E. Porter

All Rights Reserved.
No portion of this publication may be reproduced, stored in any electronic system, or transmitted in any form or by any means (electronic, mechanical, photocopy, recording, or otherwise) without written permission from the publisher. Brief quotations may be used in literary reviews.

Unless otherwise stated, all Scripture references have been taken from the King James Version (KJV) of the Holy Bible.

ISBN 10: 1945117095
ISBN 13: 978-1945117091
Library of Congress Control Number: 2016939723

For information, contact:
Soulidified Publishing LLC
Marilyn E. Porter
P.O. Box 466811
Lawrenceville, GA 30042
info@marilyneporter.com

HERSTORY Reveals His Glory

DEDICATIONS

Thank you to the following women of God for sharing your "HERSTORY" and helping other women heal:

M.E. Porter – HERstory: The Most Loved Unloved Woman in the World

Cheron K. Griffin – HERstory: The Preacher's Wife

Rev. Carma Arnette – HERstory: Married to the Secret

Angela Edwards – HERstory: I Loved Him; He Loved Crack Cocaine

Deborah Harrison – HERstory: Titanium

Kae Spencer – HERstory: A Woman Without a Reflection

Chantel Rogers – HERstory: I am an Overcomer

Michelle Flagg – HERstory: The Genesis Woman

Vernell LaMones – HERstory: Foolish Woman

Novella Robinson – HERstory: From Pain to Purpose

Gail Freeman – HERstory: Recovered & Redeemed

Naomi Smith – HERstory: Illness is **NOT** Until Death

Stephanie Whipple

HERSTORY Reveals His Glory

HERSTORY AUTHOR DEDICATIONS

From Author M.E. Porter to Juanita, Josie & Cathy.

From Author Stevii Mills to K. Mills.

From Author Famira Green to M. & F. Green.

From Author Angela Edwards to father, James Boyce.

From Author Cindy Miller to A. C. Rankins.

From Author Christina Wilson to Misha and Charity (The Sisters).

From Author Adrienne Santana to T. Santana.

From Author Tiffany Campbell to Dre and The Girls.

HERSTORY Reveals His Glory

ACKNOWLEDGEMENTS

Angela Edwards – To my loving and supportive husband, James: I thank and appreciate you.

Cindy Miller – To my coach, Marshea Mayfield: Thanks for believing in me.

Stevii Mills – Thanks for being here for a reason, season, or lifetime.

Christina Wilson – My Family (Mom, Dad and The Sisters) & GOD.

Famira Green - Thank you, God, for giving me strength to share, and my parents for the courage to be me.

HERSTORY Reveals His Glory

FOREWORD

In 2003, at her Arise! Ministry Conference, I met a humble and powerful woman of God. Her name was Marilyn. Today, that woman is my confidante, kindred spirit, soul-stirring cheerleader, and a voice of reality and revelation! The Lord has truly blessed her. We celebrate our friendship every week in what I call 'Mondays with Marilyn' – our special time together. Our lives have been parallel and powerful. We've shared the same experiences at the same time, in different spaces and places in every area of our lives; family, business, and ministry.

Marilyn has the power to pull together a community of like-minded and empowered people (especially women) to shift souls and change destinies! Her no-nonsense approach to telling the truth for the liberation of all is the fulfillment of her calling (for the truth shall surely set you free). I know that the Lord is with her! This Renaissance woman is a preacher, teacher, psalmist, innovator, and visionary!

This book is full of wisdom through experiences and transformations of life. You will laugh, cry, get angry, and be ecstatically elated at the end of each story – and none of us will ever be the same!

Thank you, M.E., for sharing the life-changing power through '**HERSTORY**'! As you say and I feel: "I love you to life, my Sista!"

Pastor Denise Elbert
Education and Empowerment Specialist
Motivationally ME

Revelation 12:11

"And they overcame him by the blood of the Lamb, and by the word of their testimony; and they loved not their lives unto the death."

About M.E. Porter

Not everyone easily shows up in the world as themselves! The masks are often plastered on in layers and people are often lost in the lies of the façade far longer than necessary. Not so with M.E. Porter. The Spiritual Guiding Light has always revealed her purpose. Amid telling a few lies, M.E. has never been untrue about who and what God has called her to **BE**.

M.E. gets down and dirty about the trials and *seeming* defeats of her life. You will be drawn into her theatrical story-telling each time she speaks. Living on the promise the Lord spoke to her many years ago, "I will never allow them to hurt you with your story", M.E. boldly and unapologetically speaks of sexual immorality, abortion, divorce, and disloyalty – to herself and others.

M.E. is a firm believer that your gifts, talents, skills, and (most importantly) the anointing of God announces you to the world, so it is a rare occasion when she functions in titles. She is a minister of the gospel, teacher, encourager, motivator, and mentor. A skilled singer and writer, M.E. stands fully in the Five-Fold Ministry and operates in the apostolic mantel that rests on her life.

Mother. Minister. Mentor. Motivator. Media Personality. Mogul-in-the-Making.

She is M.E. Porter – The Soul Shifter.

HERSTORY Reveals His Glory

Table of Contents

DEDICATIONS 3
HERSTORY AUTHOR DEDICATIONS 4
ACKNOWLEDGEMENTS 5
FOREWORD 6
About M.E. Porter 8
If God is Love, Then Who am I? 11
Born to Be Promiscuous 13
God's Whispers 21
From Defeated to DIVA 34
If God is Love, Then Who am I? 47
Jesus, My Friend Jesus 49
If God is Love, Then Who am I? 50
The Lonely Weirdo 52
From the Waterfront to the Boardroom 59
Stuck in an Identity Crisis 73
Growing in Faith 79
If God is Love, Then Who am I? 80
~~Mistaken~~ by Man, Inspired Through God 82
He Loved Me…In Reverse 91
Abuse is Not Love 98
If God is Love, Then Who am I? 99
In closing… 101
MY STORY… 103
Authors' Bios 120

HERSTORY Reveals His Glory

HERSTORY Authors' Favorite Quotes 129

M.E. Porter's Bio.. 130

HERSTORY Reveals His Glory

If God is Love, Then Who am I?
"…love is kind and thoughtful…"
M.E. Porter

I remember thinking to myself that it was so sad my uncle had passed away. After all, he had been such an intricate part of my life – perhaps the **only** man I had ever witnessed be a great father *and* a loving husband. So why don't I feel sadness for myself?

I am sad for my mom because she lost her brother.

I am sad for his children because they lost their father.

I am sad for my other cousins because they lost their uncle.

I am sad for his friends because they lost a great friend.

Oh – and his neighbors…my uncle was a great neighbor.

Perhaps the whole world will suffer at the loss of this great man – yet I feel nothing!

I am sure that some would say I had simply been in shock (or even denial) – unable to feel anything. After all, only 30 minutes had passed since my nosey neighbor barged into my auntie's bathroom – where I sat on the toilet with my pretty pink panties at my ankles – and very excitedly exclaimed that she heard my uncle had just died.

"Why is she in this bathroom?" was my first thought. *"Oh my goodness: Am I supposed to get upset and, if so, what facial expression should I be flaunting?"* As these thoughts strolled through my mind, I could already hear the devastation of the news affecting my aunt in a nearby room.

Now, this aunt was not related to this uncle. She was my dad's sister, and he was my mom's brother. They had actually dated as teenagers.

I sat there a while longer trying to decide on how I should react to the news. All the while, others came to comfort me because they were **certain** I would have a reaction to the news. I had *none*…until I forced out a deep breath and struggled to stimulate a flood of tears.

The tears never came that time – nor did they come many other times when I needed them to. I trained myself to respond with some form of a powerful emotion when horrible things happened…but the truth was that I genuinely felt nothing – and I was afraid of my nothingness.

HERSTORY Reveals His Glory

Born to Be Promiscuous
Tiffany Campbell

That glorious day when we all are revealed,
Not knowing the life ahead or the tasks to be fulfilled;
We're nourished and loved and handled with care,
Carelessly allowing future crosses to bear…

I was born to a mother - so full of life, much laughter;
A father who wasn't ready to take on the heart of a child thereafter…
The household was always kept with such love and great care.
There were rules to abide by,
An allegiance my sister and I both shared…

I was always taught at a very early age
That we are to serve a high God;
To pray and behave,
To love and respect,
To appreciate and reflect,
To learn and to grow,
To cherish all that we know,
To be right with our God,
And allow the blessings to flow…

Regardless of what is taught,
It's what a child sees
That ultimately distinguishes
Between a blessing and a disease…

HERSTORY Reveals His Glory

The hugs and the kisses,
Heart-filled terms of affection,
Smiles and giggles,
Loving arms of protection;
The handshakes and high-fives,
No matter how wise,
Doesn't prepare you for a life of demise…

At times, mommy didn't know exactly what to do
With not just one kid,
But with her two.
Family became a huge help for us,
But for me, it was an introduction to a life of mistrust…

The summers were fun,
Many memories were made;
From playing in mud
To running through a cornfield maze.
The days kept us busy,
Our mouths full of chatter,
But some evenings held a different vibe
Surfacing the question of, "What's the matter?"

The touching and teasing didn't begin all at once.
Comfort and familiarity had to set in;
It took a few months…

Many moments of disgusting and unwanted acts
Posed questions and curiosity to settle,
Eluding the fact

HERSTORY Reveals His Glory

That I was no longer innocent.
I was no longer a child;
The damage was done,
The temptation grew wild…

Confusion persisted,
Fantasy rooted itself in my head,
As evil stared me in the face
And lured me to her bed…

The attack on the soul,
And such a beautiful mind,
Makes one wonder,
"Is this all I am on the inside?"

Adults have no idea
The thoughts of a child;
Only assuming the innocence is there
And the evil is mild…

Adolescence is tricky
For those who don't know;
You grow into something,
Your feelings don't show.
You suppress all the thoughts
To fit in with the crowd,
Just to find out in the end
Memories can always be found…
The acts you deemed 'normal'
Are not normal at all,

HERSTORY Reveals His Glory

But how can you notice
When you're destined to fall?

I don't blame her, though, for the choices ahead.
Who knew what abuse swam around in her head?
It was probably a man
Or something much worse –
What us Black folks refer to as "a family curse"…

Beauty disguised the true passion I felt,
To find the reason to how I made the hearts of men melt.
My charming words would first set the tone
For the many moments I would have with them all alone…

There was nothing to fear
As I grabbed hold to control.
The strings that made me a puppet
Took hold of my soul…

In the back of my mind, there was always the thought
If the way I was acting was a result of things taught.
I was consumed with the demons
That my childhood had brought…

I grew up as a Christian.
I was in church all the time,
Praying and dancing,
Singing hymns that would rhyme;
Serving and praising,
Studying the Word of the Lord,

HERSTORY Reveals His Glory

Elders raising children on a different accord;
But yet and still, the folks of the church
Is where the most evil would ultimately lurk…

My younger years was a very confusing time,
Trying to figure out which thoughts were truly mine;
Hoping and PRAYING
For some kind of direction,
Other than knowing how to create an erection…

As I shed the skin of my adolescence,
The demon within had clearly claimed its presence.
The loss of a birth, and another unplanned
Just added checkmarks to the evil at hand…

The clouded thoughts of a girl so terribly misguided,
Needing clarity and meaning
So she can live and not hide it.
Hide the fact that she was born to be promiscuous
With a cup half-filled with the demon of lust…

The loss of my mother
Had a numbing effect;
I became unapologetic
Full of hate and neglect…

Disconnected from LOVE;
So, in the arms again I flew
To the awaiting wolves
Who seemed like they knew

HERSTORY Reveals His Glory

That my heart was heavy
And my mind was shattered:
Them, whispering sweet nothings –
Me, pretending to be flattered…

Some family and friends came to rescue me at times,
But what can you tell someone
If it's their soul they can't find?

There had to be an end,
There had to be a way
To give up the lessons
That led me astray…

So, once again I prayed to my GOD;
I cried and pleaded for Him to fix my inside.
I studied and gave myself fully to Him,
The fiery light of sin soon became dim…

I asked Him to forgive me for all that I had done
And to send me a man who would make me the one;
To make me a mother yet once again,
So that the life He had for me could soon begin…

I believed He would answer.
I gave Him a try,
Considering all that I did
Put me on a path to surely die…

HERSTORY Reveals His Glory

Through all the pain,
The tests and the trials,
The continuous searching,
The running for miles,
The hurt and the loss,
The suffering and strife,
He finally gave me
The meaning of life…

He told me to watch.
He told me to listen,
Because the love He had for me
Measured farther than I could mention…

He said that He knew my heart
Regardless of what I did –
That the fight was not mine;
That ultimately it's His…

So, finally I understood
That the life that I led
Was leading to Him –
Not to another's bed…

He helped me to forgive myself
And those who I blamed.
He gave me the chance
To better my name…

He opened my heart to accept who He is.
He gave me my children,
And I am ever so grateful He did.
He gave me my husband
Who shows unconditional love.
With all this I must give thanks to the Man up above.

Now, faith is the substance of things hoped for,
the evidence of things not seen.
Hebrews 11:1

If True Love is what you're searching for,
It's not far as it may seem.
It is closer to you than you may know;
Just look inside yourself and allow
The True Love of God to show…

HERSTORY Reveals His Glory

God's Whispers
Adrienne Santana

There are many newly-discovered freedoms at four years old. As a little girl, I reveled in mine. Having been abducted from my mother by a father who saw fit to blister and bruise my hide regularly, wiping away my tears had become part of the daily routine for my granddaddy and his sister, my Great Aunt Mary. I suppose that was why they allowed me to do pretty much *anything* I wanted – all, of course, within very broad boundaries of reason.

Taking off through the kitchen door without shoes on my feet so I could catch granddaddy early enough to feed the chickens and follow him around tugging at his shirttails asking, "Can I…Pleeeease?" proved to be of great reward. These little morning routines eventually paved the passage for my newfound freedom and love for adventure. Each night before bed, I could barely contain the excitement bubbling up inside of me as I dreamed of what the next day would hold. Climbing trees, digging tunnels through sand piles, hammering nails, painting the world blue, and eating oranges next to a fire with my 'best-est' friend, granddaddy, every evening are only a few of life's little daisies I've picked up along the way.

Obviously, no 4-year-old is absolutely happy and ecstatic about life 100% of the time. "Oh, contraire!" May the Lord forbid the day I was actually told "no" or anyone tried to lovingly explain how climbing on an old wood pile would prove too dangerous for me. Maybe my grandparents' compulsion to make me happy also had a little bit to do with my innate ability to throw an *almighty fit* – as my granddaddy described them. I was an only child then, so I can't imagine having learned how to successfully throw myself on the floor, wailing to the top of my lungs while flailing my arms and legs around. No. That, my friends, was a skill gifted by God alone through the rite of birth. Oh…and it worked – every single time!

Yes, I remember very well throwing such almighty fits. There were numerous reasons a child having gifts and talents to a prodigious degree would go through such extents. Walking the aisles through the little girls' section of JC Penney had proven to be pretty profitable. A dainty little dress with a pleated waist, seven pastel layers, and a little yellow bow adorning each layer on any other girl would have been a crying shame. So why should I have taken "no" for an answer?

My fits weren't completely materialistic. No, sir. Remember: Pain had been no stranger to me. I suppose because my father wouldn't stop in his rage until I had quit screaming, my granddaddy and Aunt Mary found it completely acceptable that I chose to use my voice so auspiciously during my tantrums – especially after having abandoned their pleas to put shoes on my feet and their constant warnings not to climb the old wood pile. After all, my well-timed screams of sheer and utter pain were what alerted granddaddy to come running with the bottle of iodine. My continued cries ensured hugs, kisses, and healing at the bottom of every bowl of ice cream.

Either way, whether monetary or emotional gains were to be had, two lessons I learned very early on in life were:

1. Healing was always *swift and sweet*; and
2. Never take "no" for an answer.

Fast forward 35 years. After having spent countless hours in therapeutic chairs and beds, I learned this: While I should never take "no" for an answer, when the occasion rises that I **speak** the word "no" myself, it should be adhered to. Yes, it took years of therapy and having thrown hundreds of almighty fits for me to realize I actually have power and authority over what happens in my life. However, the most difficult lesson through it all was realizing that not all quick fixes completely heal our wounds. Most often, emotional wounds leave the deepest scars. Some require extensive surgery – lest they consume our souls.

"What do I mean?" you ask.

Well…have you ever felt the icy chill of death's hand upon your face or the emptiness left behind as all you are is stolen by her gaze? Have you ever heard your soul cry as she glared into your eyes? Have you ever sung the song of surrender as God's glory passed by?

I have.

In that quick and quiet moment, when one becomes an adult who is faced with cleaning up the aftermath of a madman's violent and incestuous crimes, I was awakened to the fragility of life – only this time, it wasn't from the threat of my father's words, the pounding of his fist, or even at the end of his gun. No. This time, I was on my knees with my head in my hands and tears pouring down my face because *I wanted to DIE.*

As all those I loved entered my mind, I gasped for air that seemingly did not exist. With an icy vapor, their memories vanished while the truth of eternity consumed the remnants of my heart. Left in the wake of destruction was this young woman's journey and the reality of a sickly, bitter, angry soul. The very blood of my spirit – my lifeline to God – had become diseased and filthy.

Until then, I felt I had roamed the earth as 'a dead soul being tossed to-and-fro'. My faith and belief in God had been used as a tool of manipulation and deceit in justification of my father's heinous crimes against me. Much like a daisy presses through the dry and cracking ground and appears to be "a weed" in the beginning, with a broken and contrite spirit, I found myself reaching as far as my heart could reach. I searched for sorrow, fear, anger, pain, laughter, or joy. *Anything* would have been something.

Nothing came.

My life lay suspended in *nothingness* as my beginning and my ending had become one. I was 35 years old, and life had not yet begun. I felt I had always crawled beneath the feet of men, yet somehow I knew; if I could touch the hem of Christ's garment…just the part that dragged along the ground through the mire in which I lived…I knew I would be made whole.

Decades had passed since I left my father's house and there I knelt before God. My lungs began filling with tears – gut-wrenching sobs clawing their way out of my throat as they drowned out the beat of my heart, *begging* God… No, not begging: <u>*Demanding*</u>!

I know you must be saying, "…but I've been told you're not supposed to demand anything of God. It's a sin."

Well, I say, "Tell that to a 4-year-old little girl throwing an almighty fit and screaming for her life" – because that is exactly who I had become in that quick and quiet moment.

So, as I knelt on the floor of my loft all alone – screaming at God like a 4-year-old – what was God really supposed to do?

Naturally, feeling virtue fade with my tears, He did what any loving parent would do who saw their child's soul suffering: He knelt on the floor and, while allowing me to cry in His embrace, He whispered, "Daughter, thy faith hath made you whole; go in peace."

That very moment in time revealed the most important lesson I have ever learned in my life – that one moment when God seemed to have reached inside of me and taken away all my scars. I learned this: No matter what I do, what my circumstances are, or where I am in life... ***I am worthy***!

Subsequently, I call my sperm donor 'Gullob' now. I know; strange name. I never felt good about calling him anything else though, and he most **certainly** doesn't deserve to be called one of God's creations. I do, however, remember watching *Lord of the Rings* on television as a little girl. The moment my eyes fell on Gollum and I heard "*My Precious*" slither from his throat, my bones shook. I had grown up having nightmares of my 'daddy' being the devil's baby, and there he stood on national television for the whole world to see. Truth be told, I changed the name around a bit because albeit Gollum is a fictional character, to name my donor after him still seemed a bit unfair...to Gollum.

Since that great day of deliverance, I lived knowing that God met me right where I was at every moment of every day. So, four years ago upon arriving in Alabama, I knew in my heart God was bringing me full circle. I mean, why else would He lead me back to a place I had ran from 25 years earlier?

I was excited, full of life, love, and energy abound. I met the man of my dreams and fell deeper in love than I ever imagined could exist between a man and a woman. I was walking in the warmth of God's favor. I praised His name in the confidence of an unwavering belief that all was in His hands and I was exactly – as I always had been – right where He wanted me to be.

My burdens were light and my heart was filled with gladness in the assurance and belief that much of what life throws at us in the way of challenges or obstacles are only distractions. They will pass with the wind – if we would only choose to breathe and let them be. Nothing – no power above or below – could stop me. I gave absolutely no thought to my inevitable transition from beginning-to-ending-to-beginning again or what it required.

Never would I have anticipated anything being able to literally "knock me down". In my mind, it was not a possibility. I believed God knew my heart and He was aware of how terrifying physical pain and suffering were to me. He would <u>*never*</u> allow more. More than what I had already experienced would have killed me…but more did come.

Three impinged nerves at the top of my spine due to Degenerative Disc Disease didn't just bring more pain. Incomparably numerous illnesses and ailments would follow: Chronic Fatigue, Fibromyalgia, migraines lasting weeks, dizziness, a Hiatal Hernia, a couple duels with food poisoning, Tinnitus, swelling in my inner ears making it nearly impossible to hear, lumps in my neck as my salivary glands became blocked – all as my throat swelled to the point medications and food would become lodged and have to dissolve in order to go down.

My ability to dance, chase, and play with my grandchildren gradually dissolved. Eventually, seeing them came to a halt as the pain increased. My heart sank, for the blessing of having them in my life had kept me young…and without them, my spirit languished.

Since childhood, I have been compelled to encourage others and become a mirror of the inspirations and life that we all hold inside our heart. Perhaps it's been compassion and empathy for the downtrodden and heart-broken or an internal need for affection. Either way, no matter how I tried, no matter how deep the longing, my efforts and work seemed to be in vain. My own motivators and mirrors of inspiration had been taken away through my inability to *'do more and be more'*. So, in the beginning I cried... A lot!

I would wake suddenly from sleep groaning with pain and drag myself to the living room so as to not wake my husband. *One of us had to have some sleep.* I sat with my pillow in my lap...crying. My home went untouched for weeks at a time. I cried more. My husband did all the cooking and my shopping trips became his daily chore. I cried more. The added responsibilities on my husband drove steely knives of guilt through my heart. I cried more. Every good day, my announcements of 'finally getting better' would prove untrue within the hour, and failure to keep my promises flooded my heart with shame. I cried even more.

The list of ailments and doctors seemed to expand daily, as many of those days were spent flat on my back – and sometimes my face. Days, weeks, and months went by and the pain seemed to grow exponentially with every passing moment. Doctor visits were filled with tears and pleas for help.

I would sit watching the sun break through the skyline in the mornings and converse with God on the matter. I went through confusion, sadness, depression, anger, and every possible reason why this could have happened. I even blamed myself. *What had I done? Had I brought more pain on myself spiritually? Had I done someone wrong somewhere? Had I stopped hearing or listening for God's voice? Was I eating or drinking wrong? Had I injured myself at some point?* I was guilty and I knew it. I had obviously done **everything** wrong.

My constant companions' encouragement and prayers as they stood alongside me listening to my fears, questions, confusion, anger, and sadness preserved my soul from the dangers of giving up. Their love and wisdom illuminated what I knew in my heart to be true.

My healing was not only mine to have. It ran much deeper than that. I sat sobbing once again – only this time I wasn't demanding. I was **believing** because *I wanted to LIVE*!

Healing is what I believed I would receive. During the past four years, there have been many times when it would seem as though healing never came. By virtue of patience, I have come to realize that healing is what I have indeed received. Healing witnessed and seen by others is healing for the nations. Had my healing been meant for my eyes and heart alone, I would have received it immediately upon request. It would not have been allowed the time required to manifest itself to the world around me.

Truly, the challenges and obstacles life throws at us along the way are not only 'distractions'.

Blessings are all around us – God's gifts. I see them so clearly in my life and the lives of those around me. I see them because my heart has required them and is open to receive them. When I look back through my past and down the road I've traveled, I see where I was blessed beyond comprehension at times…times I never noticed because I had perceived them as *mere distractions* and had *only let them be*.

They say hindsight is 20/20. I've often asked myself, *"Why can't we have that vision now? Why does it have to be hindsight?"* I believe my adventurous quest to inspire others, combined with my explorations and search of the truth, are what brought me on this journey. God says if we ask, we will receive. Something has to make us ask questions, seek truth, and desire to encourage and inspire others. So many times I've said to God, *"I keep asking and you said I would receive…so what's up, God?"* I seriously do have conversations with Him in that manner. I wasn't only rebellious to my natural parents: **The Big Man caught the worst from me.**

Two years ago, God renewed a desire in my heart to write again. This time, my inspiration originated during my conversations with Him as we deliberated over His Scripture and its reflection upon my life. My challenge was to find beauty in the pain, fear, anger, and suffering I had experienced. More challenges were not quite the answer I was seeking from God, but as I would soon learn: Therein would lie true inspiration and encouragement – along with freedom and healing.

Suddenly, I would find myself sitting at the computer typing at what seemed like hypersonic speeds. I wrote through curtains of tears at times and often, in reading over what had been written, I found more tears rolling down my cheeks. I would sit reading – fists full of tissue – with my heart expanding through not only tears of sadness, but also tears of joy, love, and peace…and tears of freedom. My heart was being opened to receive. I knew then: If I could take every terrible moment in my life and find beauty in them, I would truly be free. I love the freedom God gives me; a place in Him where my senses seem to leave as my spirit meets with His. In the process, I have found real love, true love, and a love that fears nothing. It's a love so boundless and so consuming, it conquers and heals all that is within me.

You see, I had forgotten my worth – but God's love is immeasurable, insurmountable, and inseparable by time and space. It is the fabric from which we are made. Once again, in that quick and quiet moment, God whispered to my soul…

"Let patience make her perfect work so that you will be perfect, entire, and in want of nothing."

HERSTORY Reveals His Glory

Each year of my life has been filled with challenges, trials, and what seemed to be impossible dreams as the good fight of faith felt faint at times. Throughout my journey, my most treasured gift has been God's whispers. God's whispers are always there. They are the air I breathe and every vibration beneath my feet. They are the breaths making flutters in my heart as my husband looks into my eyes and a glimpse of myself is found in his gaze. God's whispers are the love felt between my children and me and the fierceness for which I defend and protect them. They are the compulsion and moxie to survive the unthinkable. His whispers designed the path and propelled the unquenchable love and desire that reunited my mother and me. They are the faint and sometimes painful tugs in my gut, the deafening sound of jagged stones in my chest as they cracked and crumbled amidst the silence of my tears being choked back.

I now know why it's always been hindsight. I was too busy being a mom, wife, daughter, sister, and employee. My circumstantial life was too important with all the daily duties and responsibilities. The dynamics were insane – a rat race really – and I would pray for the day I could move as far away from all that noise and "those people" as I could. I wasn't talking with God. I most certainly wasn't listening to or for Him. I was ranting, crying, and telling Him how exhausted I was – always asking Him to change my circumstances. My heart now knows why God never made that happen. Changing the world and people around me (or even my reactions to them) wouldn't have made a difference, but...*changing the heart of 'who' I am would change my world.*

HERSTORY Reveals His Glory

I had to come to a place where I sat silently listening for His voice. I'd always heard Him. His love for life and His creations surround me every day as the crickets sing for rain and leaves rustle on the trees with every cool burst of wind. However, I was seeing only half the blessing. **Hearing** His voice inside of me was required for true change to take place. He is the whispering voice of my daisies. The vibrancies and zest in life, the agony and suffering, are all-inclusively my own intricately designed blessings – each one an extraordinary and precious memory from times past. One by one, without exception, there is a separate note and chord in the song of life known as Adrienne.

There are no steps backward. Each moment is a step forward as every twist and turn, every incline and decline, has lead me from beginning-to-end-to-beginning again. Today, I wouldn't trade a single tragedy because had it not been for my darkest hour – had someone else taken my burdens – I would not know the power and glory of God as it exists in my heart and life today.

We are extensions of Him…the gateways between what flows above and below…the vessels of His infinite possibilities, eternal life, and His fantastic love. As long as we believe and listen with patience, *God's Whispers* will carry us as the wings of an eagle on the winds of time.

"My brethren, count it all joy when you fall into diverse temptations; Knowing this, that the trying of your faith works patience. But let patience have her perfect work, that you may be perfect, entire and wanting nothing. If any of you lack wisdom, let him ask of God, that gives to all men liberally, and upbraided not, and it shall be given to him."
James 1:2-5

From Defeated to DIVA
Famira Green

Today when I wake up, I wake into having GREAT days! I'm truly enjoying life and loving those surrounding me. Most importantly, I am loving the one I see in the mirror each morning. When I work with clients or speak on stage and people see the DIVA in action, I often get asked, "Have you always been this way?" The answer to that inquiry is a resounding "NO!" No, I have not always been this way. It's only by the grace of God that I've arrived at this place. Even being where I am now is a daily process of renewing my mind and keeping my perspective on life in check.

However, when I look back over my life, I can truly say that I've come a long way (as the church mothers would say). *I often think back to that young girl of my past…*

I still remember one day in the 5th grade. My dad did my hair. I was on a natural high because my ponytails were looking AWESOME! I was smiling from ear to ear as I beamed with 'Daddy's Girl' pride. While sitting in class, a group of girls asked me, "Who did your hair?" "My daddy!" I said, still beaming with that 'Daddy's Girl' pride.

Much to my surprise, one girl sucked her teeth and another girl rolled her eyes at me! They treated me as though I was lying or something. Then, it happened: The girl who rolled her eyes turned to me and said, "You got White girl hair anyway!"

I found out years later that even the teacher didn't believe me when I said my dad did my hair, so she never reprimanded the girls for their cruelty.

I remember in that moment looking down at my chocolate skin while feeling confused and instantly saddened. I went home that day and asked my mom what it meant for someone to tell me I had "White girl hair" – with an emphasis on 'good hair'. My mom's response was that I had my own hair and that everyone had 'good hair'…if they took care of it. Unfortunately, her response didn't cancel out the hurt I felt. That incident would prove to be the first of many more to come in my life with similar messages. Since that incident in elementary school, I struggled with my appearance. I was often told that my hair was "too good" for me to really be Black and that my complexion was too dark to be beautiful.

It didn't stop there, though. While in high school, I learned what the world truly thought of my chocolate skin. I had a best friend at the time who was what's considered in the African American culture as light-skinned, tall, and the equivalent of what beauty was supposed to look like – at least according to all the messages that were surrounding me. She often received compliments like "Beautiful smile", "Beautiful hair", "Beautiful this", and "Beautiful that". These became what I called 'the pretty girl compliments'. I never received those.

The compliments I received were always overly-sexualized. You see: I had curvy hips, full breasts, and a round backside. Guys would tell me I had a "banging body" and **THAT** is why they found me attractive. They would say things like "You have a sexy body", "Look at those full lips", and other offensive 'compliments' that I can't even repeat here. I began to believe that my big booty made me pretty and that it was within my physical stature that my beauty rested.

As if high school wasn't bad enough, I also had to deal with the media telling me I was inadequate, too! Take, for example, the popular movie *Coming to America*. In it, there was a prince who was set for a prearranged marriage to a beautiful chocolate-skinned woman who was overly-sexualized. Her attire placed a lot of emphasis on her body. Her dress was extremely tight and her breasts were popping out the top. To make matters worse, she couldn't think for herself. It was as if she had no brain of her own. So, the prince comes to America to find true love. While in Queens, New York, he meets two sisters: one is light-skinned, the other dark. The darker sister is portrayed as an overly-sexualized gold-digger looking for any man to make her own so he could take care of her. The lighter-skinned sister is portrayed as the wholesome, responsible one who is exactly what the prince has been looking for. That movie – and so many other messages from television, magazines, and videos – reinforced the image of the dark-skinned, overly-sexualized woman. I didn't like that.

Constantly being surrounded by those types of images everywhere I turned was truly disheartening. Even as I walked along my journey of being who I wanted to be and making decisions that were right for me, it was still a difficult path. It's like driving down a street that you KNOW is the way to get to your final destination, but all the signs say 'Wrong Direction', 'Don't Enter Here', or 'U-Turn'. You begin to second-guess yourself…and your decisions.

Though I didn't like it, I began to give in to it. I began to dress provocatively – you know…to accentuate the positive. The one thing that made me beautiful was my body. Yes, I began to gain attention; however, at the time, I didn't realize it wasn't the kind I needed or even really wanted. But hey, some attention was better than no attention!

Then, one night when I was 19 years old, the unthinkable happened. It started out so innocently; just a double-date/blind date with a friend. You know the type: My girlfriend was dating a guy and she invited me along. Her boyfriend invited a guy he knew from the college football team. We went to the movies and everything was going great. I remember my date being very attractive, attentive, and had a great sense of humor. After the movies, the four of us went back to my place and the fun continued. We were all talking and enjoying each other's company. My roommate at the time was over 21, so we decided to dabble in the liquor cabinet and have some drinks.

After drinking for a while, my friend and her boyfriend left my date and me in the living room alone. By this time, he was sitting on the floor and I was laying on the couch. He kneeled down beside me and kissed me. In that moment, I felt special. *That moment didn't last long.* He then began trying to unbutton my pants. I told him, "No. Don't touch my pants. I'm not looking to have sex with you." He looked at me and told me I was being a tease. In response, I said, "It's not like that. We just met!" In a moment that had to be a matter of mere seconds, he had scooped me up off the couch and pinned my body to the floor.

I kept asking him what he was doing and telling him no: I didn't want to go all the way. I felt his body pierce mine, and in the moment that he entered me and began to have his way, I left my body. I had a thousand thoughts crossing my mind. *Did I lead him on? Did I really tease him? Maybe I shouldn't have let him kiss me. Maybe the fact that we had a drink together in some way gave him permission to be violating my body like this.* I worried about what my friend would think if I called out. Would anyone believe me based on all that had transpired throughout the night? My shock and disappointment quickly turned to rage. I looked at him as he was on top of me and asked, "If you're not going to stop, should I get into it then?" I couldn't handle the thought of not being in control. In the moment, that was the only way I could see myself regaining control. His response back to me caused a gash in my soul. He looked right at me and said, "No. I'm done." Then, he pulled out and ejaculated on me.

With shame, horror, and disgust, I made my way to the bathroom. I locked myself in, cleaned myself up, and spent the rest of the night balled up sleeping on the floor. I cried and cried. I couldn't believe I had just been a victim of a date rape. It took me months to tell my friend what happened – and years to tell anyone else. I spent the next three years with the 'get them before they get you' mentality when it came to men.

My family had always told me I was beautiful; however, I still chose to believe the message of those around me instead of those who loved me. It was simply easier to believe the negativity because that message was louder. Every time I looked at the covers of magazines in the 90s, I would get discouraged because there was NO one on them resembling me.

That moment of honesty, self-reflection, and clarity marked the beginning of my journey to true self-confidence! I realized that the messages from the outside world – including people I was surrounded by and the media – were coming through loud and clear: You're not beautiful! You're too dark! You're only good for sex! You're NOT worthy! You're NOT enough! I was drowning in doubt and my excuses were overflowing. There was no one on the outside looking in who could make me believe my reality could be any different…not my family nor my true friends.

Several years later (in my 20s), I had what I call a "Beauty Breakthrough Moment". While sitting alone journaling (something I did often), I realized I wasn't responsible for what anyone else thought of me. In fact, it didn't matter what they thought of me! For years, I lived my life trying to live up to the expectations of others. I even dressed a certain way to please OTHER PEOPLE. In that "Beauty Breakthrough Moment", I realized the only person I had to please was MYSELF. The only opinion that mattered was my own.

Once I decided I would no longer live my life according to the lies or the media hype of what beauty was supposed to look like, I found it absolutely necessary to create my own beauty standards. I didn't know what that would look like, but I had to start somewhere. What did I do? I created my own #BeautyOUTLoud mantra to speak to what I felt a woman of beauty truly was. It would be the only way I could move forward in my progress. Without it, I would have continued to beat myself up because I didn't resemble all the portraits of beauty that surrounded me.

Also, as I became more self-aware and found my voice, I began to filter through my clothes. While going through my closet, I realized an amazing truth: I came face-to-face with the attire that fed right into the stereotype of the overly-sexualized dark-skinned woman and the lies I had been told about my body equaling my beauty. I had dresses that fit my body so tight, they looked as if they were painted on. My cat suits were so snug, they looked like second skin. My blouses were cut so low, they exposed my deep cleavage. When I thought about it, I didn't buy those pieces because I liked them: I bought them because I believed that's how I had to dress to get the men's attention. Filtering through my closet showed me that I needed to continue to work on myself.

I began to ask God why this had happened to me. Why would He make me this way – someone so unwanted and not beautiful? It was then that I was led by the Holy Spirit to the Bible and the verse of Psalm 139:14 that reads, "*I will praise thee; for I am fearfully and wonderfully made: marvelous are they works; and that my soul knoweth right well.*" He also led me to the passage that would become my favorite of the Bible and still is to this day: Psalm 27:1-4: "*The Lord is my light and my salvation; whom shall I fear? The Lord is the strength of my life; of whom shall I be afraid? When the wicked, even mine enemies and my foes, came upon me to eat up my flesh, they stumbled and fell. Though an host should encamp against me, my heart shall not fear: though war should rise against me, in this will I be confident. One thing have I desired of the Lord, that will I seek after; that I may dwell in the house of the Lord all the days of my life, to behold the beauty of the Lord, and to enquire in His temple.*"

There were very clear lessons I had to learn in that moment, with one being that I could not play the victim – despite anything I had endured. I had to do the difficult thing and take responsibility for my actions in the moments. I learned that I'm only responsible for my own actions and not the actions of others. So, it was my choice to decide how I would view any situation that would come my way.

I learned that life is about *PERSPECTIVE*! Perspective is defined as a particular attitude toward or way of regarding something; a point of view. That means we can **choose** the attitude we have towards anything that happens to us. We can **choose** to be negative or positive. We can **choose** to love or hate. We can **choose** to be paralyzed or move forward. We can **choose** to believe the lies or know the truth.

No matter what the world says about my chocolate skin, **I choose to believe the truth:** I'm fearfully and wonderfully made. Whether or not every man I encounter only sees me for my body, I can choose to know the truth: I'm so much more than my body. Even in the situation of the date rape, I could choose to stay negative and hate him – which would keep me paralyzed and unable to go on with my life. *I did just that for a while, but then I made the decision to choose the opposite.* I chose to hate the action and not the person. I chose to see the positive by seeing how strong I really am despite all that comes against me. I chose to not remain paralyzed by my anger. I chose to let it go so that I could move forward with my life.

So, as you read this, please know that you have choices to make. After you've cried and released yourself to feel the pain of whatever has happened to you, it's the only thing left to do. No matter what you choose, it's a choice all the same. In this very moment, I invite you to take a deep breath and say out loud: ***I CHOOSE LIFE!*** There is power of life or death in the tongue, and you're the one who speaks the most over your own life. Know that you can speak life into every area of your life. Choose to be positive, tap into your Godly joy, and always move forward – even if your moving forward is a crawl on some days. Trust me; I understand it's not easy and that most days it's easier to be negative than it is to be positive. You must CHOOSE to push through it. Your power is in the choice.

Remember that it matters how you **SHOW UP** in this world! Just as someone reading this book has been waiting for each of us that are a part of this amazing project to show up, someone is waiting on you! It's time for you to move beyond the pain of the past and affirm your presence in the world! This is the place of power that each one of us must come to. What does it mean to affirm a thing? Affirm means to "state as a fact; assert strongly and publicly". Therefore, to affirm your presence in the world means to **SHOW UP** in strength and with boldness in the *WORLD*.

Whatever the size of the stage you were born to occupy, you must show up as the 'Star of the Show'! I don't care if your stage is in front of one person or millions, you are still designed to **SHOW UP**! Often, we get caught up in the size of our stage instead of placing the focus on where it should be: on those we are meant to touch. The size is not significant; the transformation of those watching us is. You may only be on this planet to touch *ONE* person, but that very person who's assigned to you may be the *ONE* person who is meant to go on to touch the lives of billions. Without you doing your part, you interrupt the flow of life.

There is one thing that has ALWAYS stuck with me out of all the things Jesus spoke on this earth; it's when He tells His disciples, *"I tell you the truth, anyone who believes in Me will do the same works I have done, and even greater works, because I am going to be with the Father"* (John 14:12). I'm here to let you know that we are ALL vessels from which miracles are meant to manifest for us and THROUGH us for others!

For all of those who are waiting for the business portion of this story, it's simply this: You can't get aligned without aligning ALL parts of you and everything that is attached to you. Grasp that, and even in your business you will **SHOW UP**! I want to share the following quote with you:

"Vulnerability is about showing up and being seen. It's tough to do that when we're terrified about what people might see or think."
~ Brene Brown ~

I want to encourage you to allow yourself to be vulnerable. It's in the vulnerability that you will recognize your own strength. Once you gather your strength, you'll operate in your true power – all because you finally realize that how you **SHOW UP** matters! Tell your story as I have told mine today. It's at this point in life that you will reap your COMPLETE harvest – the harvest that God speaks of in John 10:10:

"The thief does not come except to steal, and to kill, and to destroy. I have come that they may have life, and that they may have it more abundantly."

It's time for you to reap your *COMPLETE* harvest, so **SHOW UP AND STAND OUT**!

The battle for my self-worth was necessary to find the DIVA within me. I was able to move from "Defeated to DIVA" by making the decision to do so. I know that in writing this, I make it seem easier than it may feel to you in this moment. Trust me: It's not as hard as you think. Know that it's the pain of your situation – a trick of the enemy – that makes you think that you'll never come back from it. However, we must look at the truth of the matter. That truth is this:

"And we know that all things work together for good to them that love God, to them who are called according to His purpose."
Romans 8:28

HERSTORY Reveals His Glory

ALL includes the bad, traumatic, uncomfortable, and tragedy. In the truth, find strength to carry on. Step into the position of the DIVA **you** were created to be. Walk in your purpose and do so with your head held high! Write the book you're meant to write. Start the business and help the people you are destined to help. Live the life you are designed to live!

That is the mantra I live by. It is an everyday process, but I continue to walk it out because I know that by doing so, I will encourage others to do the same. I hope that on this day, the person who I have encouraged is YOU!

**SHOW UP, STAND OUT,
AND CHANGE THE WORLD!**

Stand tall and walk out your purpose. I know you can do it! I believe in you! I see the change happening already, DIVA!

Repeat after me:
I AM COURAGEOUS AND I LIVE MY DESTINY!

If God is Love, Then Who am I?
"…it does not rejoice at injustice…"
M.E. Porter

Thoughts raced through my mind as I sat in a cold, colorless room, waiting for the abortionist (ok…perhaps *doctor* is a kinder description) to enter and carry out this very necessary deed. The odd thing was this: The longer I sat there waiting, the more I began to question the need for ridding myself of the child growing in my womb. I recall thinking, *"Damn it! This is taking so long!"* Some years later, I realized the long wait is intentional – to give the mother the opportunity to make a different choice. I did not make another choice. On December 10, 1995, I relaxed my body on a cold, hard, uncomfortable table, placed my feet in stirrups, and experienced the excruciating pain of my child being sucked from my womb – yet outside of the physical pain, *I felt nothing.*

I reasoned with myself as to why I had no emotional response to the loss of life that had taken place. Perhaps it had been the best possible option and, therefore, no sadness or grief was necessary. Or maybe I hadn't allowed myself to become attached to the idea of having a 2nd child, so there was no valid cause to feel anything other than relief. ***But what if I was supposed to feel something?*** I asked myself this question: *"Who does this kind of thing and does not feel **any** remorse?"* Then, an even *greater* question came to mind: *"Why didn't I love that child enough to keep it?"* And then the *next* question arose: *"Why don't you love anything?"*

HERSTORY Reveals His Glory

There was that nothingness again, and it was even more terrifying than my first acknowledgement of it.

HERSTORY Reveals His Glory

Jesus, My Friend Jesus
Marlowe Scott © 1995

What a friend we have in Jesus;
He all our sins and grief will bear.
Our friend, Jesus, came and left Someone special
When He ascended to His Father in the air!

The Comforter, the Holy Spirit,
Surrounds each of us every day and everywhere;
Because our Beloved Counselor and Friend, Jesus,
Left the Holy Spirit here – when He joined His Father in the air!

But wait – Do you really know my friend, Jesus?
Does He all your burdens bear?
Are you really ready to meet and greet Him
When He ascends again – coming down through the air?

If not, then I invite you today to receive Him
And enjoy the friendly, bountiful love I share
With our Lord and Savior, Jesus Christ,
Who reigns in Heaven with God – up there in the air!

Come quickly! Praise and celebrate with me!
A Friend who loves unconditionally, without compare;
His name is Emanuel – Wonderful Jesus, be ye ready to meet Him
When He comes again from Glory – shouting through the air!

If God is Love, Then Who am I?
"...it is not provoked..."
M.E. Porter

I could faintly hear my mother screaming, "***Marilyn, I didn't raise you this way!***" Her voice brought me back to myself – for a moment I had drifted off into such a deep place of rage, I could not see nor hear anything or anyone for a moment. As I came back to myself, I quickly realized I had punched my aunt in the face…yes, my mother's sister – not a play aunt. Not only had I punched her, I had done it in the presence of her two children and my own child! In the span of roughly 10 seconds, my mind had become fully aware of the situation – yet I felt ***nothing***. **No** remorse. **No** shame. **No** regret. **No** need for repentance. The nothingness had reared its ugly head once again, and this time it had become my friend.

The memory of my mother's conversation with me that night is clear – her words remain crystal clear even some 22 years later – yet the only absolute memory I have of my own reaction is a cold stare. I remember just looking at my mom as she stood in front of me chastising me, and the thought that ran through my mind was: *"Please lady: Don't make me knock **you** out, too!"* In that moment in time, I was horrified at the very notion of doing so, but nothingness and I were bosom buddies in that moment. I can only thank God for His divine presence – lest my mother may have fallen victim to my alliance with nothingness.

If there was anyone on the planet who I 'thought' I loved, it was my mother; but in a moment of severe nothingness, there rested a question of my ability to love anyone at all – including the beautiful 2-year-old child of mine who had been witness to that horrible scene.

The Lonely Weirdo
Christina "Chris Dannie" Wilson

Since I was a very young child, my life always seemed to be just a little harder than others around me – especially my sisters (the oldest one, to be exact). The family – not just my mom, dad, and sisters, but the **entire** family (including close friends) – would make jokes about it. Even when things went wrong around the house and I was not present, someone would jokingly say, *"Christina did it!"*

It was never a joke to me.

My sisters and I did things together that we knew my mom would flip out about (and I do mean flip **out**), but they would very quietly slip away, leaving me to be the one to get caught and incur the full blame for our antics. As a matter-of-fact, there were many times they actually got caught, too; yet I would still get the full force of the punishment. I tried not to take it personally, but I must confess: After years went by of this same outcome, I began to feel very alone and very unloved.

HERSTORY Reveals His Glory

    Okay. I will admit: I am different. I will even admit that I tried very hard not to be so weird (as my family – not really my family…more like my *mom* would call me), but the more I tried to fit in or be like the older sister who seemed to be nearly perfect – the weirder I became! We would laugh about how I was the weird one and nobody ever understood me. Yeah, they always laughed, but I wasn't laughing at all. In fact, there were tears at the edges of my lashes very often. As much as I wanted to believe their words were just a joke, I knew that behind every joke was some truth – and the truth was that I was alone.

    One would think that my story is not valid because the *other* truth of my life is that I've always had everything I needed: shoes, clothes, a nice home, food, family, and, most importantly, a sound Christian foundation. Yes, I had everything; yet as a child, I always felt as if I had nothing.

    Imagine having a person in your life who was always in the limelight. I mean pretty – that beautiful kind of pretty – a very strong and physically-fit body, she could sing, she was athletic, had what seemed like millions of friends, and every boy in town liked her. It seemed as though she could do anything! I believed she could fly! Oh, did I mention that she played an instrument so well that she actually became the band captain? No teachers had a bad word to say about her – and she knew how to get around my mom like a pro. This person was my older sister. With her around, "Christina the weirdo" didn't stand a chance! I wanted to hate her, yet I was totally fascinated with her. I mean, this is MY big sister! I bragged about her everywhere to everyone, but as I grew older, it was not enough for me to just be 'Misha's little sister'.

Oh, but wait: My sister was not the **only** one casting a great shadow over me. There was this mom who was then and still is absolutely amazing and highly-respected by everyone – even people who don't really like her. I hated being in the shadows…especially of my mom. Although I tried to mimic my big sister, it was really mom's footsteps that made me feel paralyzed.

The real story developed from watching the two of them bond – as if I didn't even exist. Mom would spend hours working with my sister and her friends creating a really cool girl group – which my sister was the lead singer…OF COURSE. I will admit this one thing, though: My sister can sing and the group was good! If they had really wanted to be famous, I am certain my mom would have gotten them there. Mom never missed **any** of my sister's band concerts (I, however, was not so lucky). Mom was always talking to her making sure her life was great (I, however, was not so lucky). Mom never failed to smile when anyone said anything about her oldest child…yeah, my big sister (I, however, was not so lucky). Mom was always at her track meets and events – even if it meant not being with her middle child on her birthday. I specifically recall the time my sister's band went to Disney – and the day they left was my birthday. I remember wanting my mom to stay…*to choose me just that one time*…but she hopped on that Greyhound with my big sister and drove off into the sunset.

*Sidebar: Don't get me wrong. There is no parent in this world who could ever begin to TRY to compare to the mother God has blessed me with. I find myself thanking God for her sometimes – multiple times a day. So, if you are reading this and are beginning to think ill of M.E. Porter, I must request that you stop…**right now!***

Although my mother was a great parent (and my sister was and still is a great sister, by the way), I always had these thoughts in the back of my mind: *Why doesn't she acknowledge me the same way she does my sister? Why doesn't she love me the way she loves her? Why doesn't my mom like me?* It seemed like nothing I did was right. I was always wrong. Then, my dad left – the one who had always been my advocate. No one asked me if a divorce was the right thing to do. As much as I trusted him, he never confessed to me that our family was breaking up because of his actions. So, I decided in my own mind that it was my mom's fault that my daddy was leaving our home. I wondered to myself: *Why doesn't she like us?*

Once dad was gone, I was really alone. He never quite figured out how to do much more for me and my sisters other than spend money. He spoiled us. Anything we asked for, we had it. I remember once telling my mom that she was weak (*thank **God** I am still alive*) because even after my dad moved out, she still allowed him to parent – and that seemed really stupid to me. I hated her for being so darn **weak**!

One day, after they divorced, my two sisters and me were in the house (yes, there is another sister involved – she is the younger sister, which makes me the middle child). My mother came out of her room to fuss about stuffed animals and suddenly busted out crying because of all the pain she was feeling – and in that moment, I just knew that those tears were because of everything I had done wrong. I had fought, stole, lied, and treated everyone around me like I cared nothing about them – because that's how I felt. Now, not only was my mom in pain: I really felt like I did not have the support of either of my parents.

In fact, I was alone.

That was when I began to hate my older sister. She had everything I didn't have. She had my mom. I would walk around school every day making others laugh and making them believe I was enjoying life every day; yet there was a perpetual cry in my belly. No one – and I do mean *no one* – understood how I felt. I cried myself to sleep so many nights just wondering why, if I'm supposed to be so great and powerful in the world like so many people said, why did I feel like I could die and no one's life would be changed?

Sidebar: Now, let me pause for just a moment. My family had good times. We have memories and traditions that I respect and love more than anything. Without them, I wouldn't be able to pursue the career that I would like to be a part of. I wouldn't be able to attend college at The Alabama State University and major in the love of my life: theatre. I love my family. We have laughs that only we could ever even imagine to understand. There are songs that bring back memories of wonderful times. I've overcome many of the problems I had with my mother through talking to her and prayers to Christ.

My only outlet – ever – even before I knew that I wanted to act, was writing. Through said outlet, I became someone else, seeing life through the eyes of a person I created. That's how I stayed sane. Many times, I considered suicide. Many times, I considered taking away the most precious gift God gave to me because of my inability to understand that to get where I want to be in life, I had to go through some things to prepare me for what was to come. It took me so long to get that through my hardheaded skull. When I tell people this story, they always assume I'm looking for sorrow and pity, but I'm not. I tell it because I know there's some young child out there who wants what I want in life; to change the world. They won't be able to break out of what they're going through until they hear what I have to say. I believe one day I will help a child – someone who feels the way I felt. He or she will have a breakthrough and know what I know now.

HERSTORY Reveals His Glory

I am a phenomenal young woman. As I look back over my life, I see things from a more elevated view. My mom – the woman who I declared just one short year ago did not love me – in fact had secretly built me into a powerful woman. I find myself emerging as a leader. I hear her in my head leading, guiding, and making sure that I stand firm in the world as myself. I know now that the things I hated most about my mom are the things that prepared me for abundant life. Even when she would make me sit still with my hands on my lap for hours (*it seemed **so** cruel at the time*), now – as an actress – I find myself able to be calm and patient in the most frazzling situations because my mom would sit me down and whisper, *"You are not in trouble, Christina. I just need you to know how to control yourself."* Who knew that those little training exercises would be such a blessing to me now?

My big sister is **still** fabulous. She has gone on to become an officer in the military. Thank God I no longer feel the need to mimic her. I can only be a soldier for the Lord! My younger sister is actually quite amazing as well. She is a talented, beautiful young lady with her own set of weirdness going on – and I love her for it.

As for me, my story continues. I am only 18 years old – but I am expecting great things for my future. This is my story…for now.

Stay tuned!

HERSTORY Reveals His Glory

From the Waterfront to the Boardroom
Gail Freeman

My name is Gail N. Freeman. I am a 53-year-old Black female. I was born to Lee and Beatrice Pipkin in 1962. I am the youngest of five children: two brothers and two sisters. Two are yet living; myself and my eldest brother. We were a traditional two-parent family – until the sudden loss of our father in 1967. My uncle – my mother's brother – packed us up in his old, beat-up, lime green and white Chevy pickup truck (like the Beverly Hillbillies) and moved us across the Delaware River from the big city of Philadelphia, Pennsylvania to the rural country town of Mount Holly, New Jersey. I propped myself up on my knees and watched as Philadelphia slowly faded away. At some point, I noticed that my very special rocking chair fell off the back of the truck. I pleaded with my uncle and aunt to stop and pick it up, but we continued to drive on.

From that day forth, my life as I had known it – the loving, caring, and nurturing one – would be changed forever.

HERSTORY Reveals His Glory

About a year after making the move to New Jersey, my mother died from kidney failure. My brother, sister, and I were moved yet again to my uncle's and aunt's home in the most rural part of Mount Holly called Bucktoe. I didn't know it then like I know it now: I was living in paradise. The community wasn't very large. It consisted of ten houses: my grandparents', four of their children, and four other families. It was a close-knit community where everyone knew everyone or was somehow related. The development itself was nestled down at the end of Church Street right off of Rancocas Road. The Delaware River ran alongside my grandparent's home. There were multiple paths through the woods that ran from house to house. My grandfather was a farmer, and his children and grandchildren tended the land. The uncle I lived with was a pig farmer. We never went hungry. Yes, those were the "good, old days". Everything seemed so quiet and ordinary – but the things that were happening in our home were not quiet...*nor were they ordinary.*

There was a lot of physical, sexual, and mental abuse going on behind closed doors. Growing up in a household with six children likely left my aunt and uncle under more stress than they knew how to handle. My uncle coped with life's misfortunes by feeding his gambling addiction and running around on my aunt. My aunt, on the other hand, handled things her way: by lashing out on us children.

The physical abuse was the most tolerable because the feelings associated with that type of abuse were short-lived and inconsistent. My aunt mainly beat me when my uncle would beat her. As wrong as that logic was, it may have been the only release she ever knew. For example, if things in the house were out of place, my aunt would beat me severely. I was the main target for her abuse – likely because I was the youngest and the easiest to intimidate. My uncle was rarely home, but when he was, once in a while he would beat us, too. *I know now that they did the best they could and only mimicked how they were raised.*

The sexual abuse, however, was degrading, embarrassing, shameful, and just plain nasty. I hated the way his big, heavy body would press mine into the bed. It felt like I couldn't move or breathe. I hated the way the sweat would drop off of him as my body would become soaked from his sweat. I hated the way he smelled: musty and old. I didn't want any part of it, yet it was a part of my daily routine.

My routine consisted of going to school, coming home to clean the house, having sex with one or both of my male cousins, eating dinner, and then going to bed – just to do the same thing all over again the next day. I tried to tell my aunt what was happening, but she accused me of being promiscuous. *Can you imagine a 9-year-old being promiscuous – without being taught those things?* Not only was I being molested; so was my older sister.

HERSTORY Reveals His Glory

As a result of my sister being molested, she had a son whose name was Keith. Keith was my nephew **and** my 2nd cousin. *He was later killed in a home invasion in Philadelphia.* I carried that shame and guilt around for years – not understanding that it wasn't mine to carry. Years later (through therapy), I learned the shame and guilt were stopping my spiritual growth. I needed to let it go.

The most damaging of the three types of abuse I endured was the mental abuse. That type of abuse shapes one's thinking for years to come. I have not lived in my aunt's house for over 40 years, and I **just** finished therapy a year ago. Even still, I battle with the names my aunt used to call me:

Fat. Black. Ugly Alfred Hitchcock lip. Cry baby. You make me sick. You are nothing and you will never be anything. Nobody wants you. I don't even want you, but I am stuck with you. You are a liar and a thief. I can't stand you.

Those are the images and feelings that have been with me for most of my life. Those are the feelings of low self-esteem, no self-worth, uselessness, hopelessness, and despair that can creep up at any given moment and rob me of my peace and joy if I don't stay vigilant over my feelings.

I remember overhearing a conversation my mother had with my uncle. She said to him, "Whatever you do, please don't separate my children."

The first chance my aunt had, she did just that.

My brother was signed into the military at age 17, my sister was sent to foster care after having her son, and I was left to care for my nephew/cousin. My aunt kept custody of him for the same reason she kept us: the money. Every time my nephew cried, I received a beating. Every time my uncle stayed out all night, I received a beating. Every time my uncle beat my aunt, I received a beating.

I lived with my aunt and uncle until age 13. By that time, I had simply had enough. I was tired. I made a decision that I was not going to be beaten anymore. I was not having sex with my cousins anymore. I was done with cleaning the house like Cinderella. That 'fairytale' had to come to an end.

I remember the moment like it was yesterday. It was a Thursday night, and again, my uncle was out and about. My aunt told me to go down into the basement to retrieve some canned goods. Admittedly, I was being stubborn and defiant. I didn't **feel** like obeying. I was at my end…***but I didn't deserve to be pushed down the cellar stairs!*** I remember thinking to myself, *"Whatever she does to me…however long she beats me…I will not break! I will not cry!"*

Another part of the physical abuse 'routine' included the gathering of my own switch. On this day, I **chose** to march outside to the cherry tree and break off the longest switch I could find – a decision made on my own. I brought it into the house and immediately handed it to my aunt. The beating began – but I didn't cry! I stood there and withstood her beating until the switch broke into tiny pieces. When there was no more switch, she grabbed the curtain rod from the closest window and finished beating me with it. The rod caught me in the corner of my eye. When I woke the next morning, my eye was black and swollen – but still, I did not cry.

That morning (after the brutal beating), I dressed for school and rehearsed in my head what I was going to tell my teacher. I ended up telling her the truth: I was abused by my aunt and wanted to go to foster care with my sister. The system **DID** send me to foster care…but not with my sister. I bounced around for five years at different foster homes. Each home I lived in carried the same theme: *"You are only here because of the money, not because we love you or that you need love."* The foster "parents" made it plain that their services were only for monetary gain.

I never found my sister in the foster care system. I saw her again when I tried to seek refuge with her, and once more after that when she died from complications associated with diabetes.

I had a long, hard struggle trying to care for myself in young adulthood. I never had a childhood – and I surely didn't have a clue on how to be an adult. I went to live with my brother, but he took advantage of me just as the others did. I was only a source of income for him and his family. He manipulated me into signing my social security checks (benefits from my father) over to a mortgage company so he could purchase a house. He eventually lost the house to foreclosure.

I was 18 years old, full of fear and anger, and desperately looking for someone – anyone – to love me. I failed to understand that I first needed to love myself. All of that "other" stuff was in the way, though…you know the stuff: low self-esteem, low or no self-worth, self-pity, depression, and mental illness – just to name a few.

I started receiving my own social security benefits and was living with friends in a rural part of Browns Mills, New Jersey. I ended up meeting and hanging out with people who liked to party. I remember taking my first drink. It made me feel all warm and fuzzy inside. It made me feel special – like I was a part of the cool crew. It helped me say things I couldn't say when sober. It helped me stand up for myself. I could protect myself because I would fight at the drop of a hat. Yes, alcohol was the best thing since sliced bread!

My life quickly went downhill. I really don't know what happened. What I did know was that I was drinking way too much, but I couldn't stop. When I drank, all was well with the world. When I was sober, all was not. So, I drank more and more alcohol. What started as a weekend-only event would then last all week. I was hanging out in bars, so I became connected with people who used and sold drugs. Eventually, I earned the title of one of their best customers. I stole and did a lot of other things that went against my morals and values to support my growing habit.

I caused a lot of unrest and uneasiness all around me, but the greatest devastation was to my relationship with the God I serve – coupled with the harm I caused myself as a result of the decisions I was making.

I was suffering from the disease of addiction. At the time, I didn't know what addiction was or even that I was suffering from it. It's such an insidious disease. I didn't realize it was attacking me until it was too late and the damage was already done.

I would get jobs, but couldn't keep them. I would get involved in relationships, but I couldn't participate in them. I would get apartments, but couldn't maintain them. Eventually, I ended up homeless – bouncing from house to house. Survival-mode had me oftentimes shoplifting to pay for a place to live or food to eat. Every time things turned bad – meaning I had absolutely nowhere to live – I would hitchhike to a truck stop to catch a ride to another state while trying to start my life all over again. I lived in shelters, would get a job, find a place to live, get a new boyfriend…and start using drugs again.

HERSTORY Reveals His Glory

That vicious cycle lasted for over 35 years of my life.

Near the end of my drug addiction, I found myself homeless and living on the Camden Waterfront in New Jersey. My new "home" became the big, white, cold slab of concrete called 'The Cotillion'. My "bed" consisted of two blankets. The Cotillion's primary purpose was to provide a place to relax while enjoying the waterfront view, but it served as my home for a few months. The tourists would come, relax, and casually dine there. I would watch them throw away food and, as soon as the coast was clear, I would pick the "cleanest" food out of the trash to eat.

Only by God's grace, I would wake in the morning, roll up my two blankets, and walk up the hill to Frank's Place (a drop-in center for the homeless). While there, I would pick some clothes off the rack, take a shower in their old, rusty stall, then call the van to go to my outpatient MICA (Mentally Ill Chemical Abuse) group. I would stay at group until 4 p.m. then get dropped off at the transportation center. I would eat dinner at the soup kitchen, go to the liquor store to panhandle for beer and cigarettes, then walk back to the waterfront…just to do the same things all over again the next day.

Through it all, God had His hand on my life. Although fear was with me constantly, no harm came near me. I had finally reached the point in my life where I didn't want to live like that any longer. I began to utilize the government agencies around me and started looking for a place to live. Once again, God showed up and showed out. I found a place in the heart of the city. At the time, I was separated from my husband. When I moved into my apartment, we reconciled.

Needless to say, I thought I was well and had it all together. Unfortunately, I picked up using drugs again. As a direct result, my first husband dropped dead right in front of me. On that day, he apologized to me for getting me caught up in the drug game again, excused himself from the table, and went into the bedroom. A couple of minutes later, I followed him. When I entered the room, he was having a severe seizure on the bed. I called 911. The EMTs told me he didn't have a heartbeat when they took him out of the house. As we turned the corner in the ambulance, his heartbeat returned. He lived three more days…then he died.

I continued to use for another three years. Eventually, I met and married my current husband, George Freeman. We used drugs together until God intervened in our lives. George was sent to prison and I joined a 12-Step Program. I managed to get clean. I moved out of the city and into the suburbs – but nothing had really changed except my address. My thinking definitely didn't change. I stayed clean for a while…until my husband came home from prison. You guessed correctly if you thought, "*She went back to using*". There was something very different about the experiences that time: There was no more pleasure in it. I would put the drugs in the apparatus, ingest them – and go **straight** to paranoia *times 100*.

The drugs and alcohol had turned on me! They no longer did what they used to do for me in the beginning – that warm, fuzzy feeling that left me feeling like I didn't have a care in the world. My new reality was that my whole life was crumbling all around me.

It was a struggle trying to stop using. It felt next to impossible. I know it didn't happen of my own might. I know this because I stopped many times, but couldn't stay clean. I would always pick up the habit again. It would start with a job, going to school, getting into a relationship, and/or finding a place to live – all the while thinking I was well again. I had no God in my life. I was material-centered and not God-centered. Eventually, the use of drugs led me to become a homeless panhandler on the street corners and eating out of trash cans…again.

I believe God allowed me to go through all of those events to help me believe in His power. In March 2009, God reached down and pulled me out of the lions' den.

One day, I was completely out of my mind. I felt like the only way to stop using drugs and alcohol would be suicide. In the past, I had glimpses of how I would do it…but this time, I was serious. I had a plan. I was on my way to the waterfront to jump in the river – knowing I don't know how to swim. The same waterfront that was once my home was about to be my grave.

Once again, God intervened. A voice spoke to me and urged me to go into the 12:00 p.m. 12-Step meeting. Against everything in my conscience, I went. It felt like I was having an out-of-body experience – as if my feet were moving without my permission (much in the same way I would move when I was looking for drugs). I was being governed by a force, but that time it was a positive force…not a negative one.

Although I looked bad, smelled bad, and had a bad attitude, I did not receive the rejection I thought I was going to receive when I entered the meeting. Instead, I received unconditional love. They hugged me, told me how glad they were to see me, and assured me that everything would be okay. I had been broken down to my lowest point. It needed to happen that way.

Thank God for the gift of desperation! I have been clean since 2009.

In November 2013, I decided to give back to the homeless community and wanted to distribute gift bags for the Thanksgiving holiday. As I attempted to gather donations for them, it became apparent that no one wanted to assist me. I was very distraught. I wondered how people could be so cold towards other human beings. *"Why won't they help me?"* I wondered. My church didn't support me, either. I received guidance in the form of a suggestion from someone very dear to me. She simply asked, "Why don't you ask the women you are already connected to?"

From that conversation, *Just Us Girls Camden County – A NJ Nonprofit Corporation* was born. Although the corporation's name is *Just Us Girls*, it must be noted here that we service more than women: We serve our homeless, mentally-challenged, and senior communities. *Just Us Girls* is actually named in honor of the women I am connected to. It is one of the most rewarding and fulfilling endeavors I have ever been a part of.

HERSTORY Reveals His Glory

I know what it is like to enter a shelter or drop-in center and be able to take a shower with a soufflé cup full of soap. I know what it is like to care for someone in a facility and can't find two socks that match. Thank God for the shelters, but they don't always have the toiletries and some of the most basic of human needs to accommodate their clients.

To date, we service three facilities on a monthly basis through the generous donations of others. In February 2015, we received our 501c3 tax-exemption status. We can now service our targeted communities on a much larger scale.

I have used my experiences of being homeless, drug-addicted, suffering from mental illness, living in shelters, and working with the elderly to form *Just Us Girls*. My heart's desire is to give back what was so freely given to me in hopes of helping at least one person. I will let them know that if God could save a person like me – one who has been through **ALL** of the aforementioned experiences – then He could do the same for them…and for you.

I am Gail N. Freeman: CEO of *Just Us Girls*. I came from the waterfront and now serve in the boardroom.

Stuck in an Identity Crisis
Stevii Mills

The truth of the matter is I did not know my story was where God shows His glory in my life. I did not know that my mistakes and mishaps were a platform for God to show up in His perfect brilliance. I did not know that everything in my life served a purpose for people to become even more knowledgeable about God's grace and mercy.

We are truly God's representatives here on earth. We are the ones He has positioned to get His message through to the people we encounter each and every day. Glory is defined as magnificence; great beauty. When people look at you, they should see God's glory running through you. They may not even know what to call it, but they know there is *something* different about you.

The Bible teaches that we are God's handiwork. He has taken His time to create every detail that we embody.

Who am I? I am Stevii Aisha Mills. I am the woman who was once stuck in an identity crisis. I did not want to be Stevii. I wanted to be Stephanie, Samantha, Stacy, or any other name that did not draw as much attention for a female. I wanted to have a 'Plain Jane' name that would be easy to pronounce and would not lead to questions such as, "Did your dad want a son?"

Ever since I was born, I stood out. The moment my parents put my name on my birth certificate, I became someone the world has never seen before. I spent most of my life being who I thought I needed to be for other people. I wanted to blend in so much that I often stood out like a very sore thumb. I felt like the more I blended in, the easier life would be. I truly wanted to be like everyone else.

I was hindering God's glory from being seen through me because I was not allowing it to be seen fully. God – being the phenomenal God that He is – was still shining through me, but I, in my ignorance, did not realize my idiosyncrasies were His brilliance. The fact that I was the only one who was like me was not by accident. God's people are a peculiar people. It was an abomination against God that I was trying to hide my light under a bushel.

I did the things everyone else did. I did it the right way. I went to school – all the way from kindergarten through graduate school. Yes, I collected more accolades than shoes and clothes. *The funny thing about that is I **love** shoes and clothes.* However, I felt like I had to do things that would make me look great on paper: I had to have life experiences that would give me the recognition I craved instead of the rejection I often felt was coming into my life.

I was recognized for being accepted to the only university I ever applied to. I was recognized by being on every ministry in the church that I attended. I was even recognized for working at some of the most well-known companies and corporations. Yes, my resume was awesome! There was a problem, though: I was not happy. In fact, I was making myself sick because I was stressed out by being in environments that were not created for me.

I felt rejected by not receiving in return the love I was giving to men who I was trying to magically turn lust into love with. They were all handsome, intelligent, creative, and more – everything the books and media told me to go after. They were not looking for relationships…or at least not with **me**. They were looking for me to be their *friend*, their *chick on the side*, or their *financier*. I was trying to be the one they put the beautiful diamond ring on and took home to their families. I wanted to have a wedding that would make all of the society pages – and maybe even be featured in a magazine or two!

What was the turning point for me? It was working a job I hated going to every day. I loved the salary that directly deposited into my bank account on time every pay period. I loved the benefits that allowed me to see the best doctors and dentists that my money could buy. I even loved the people I worked with. The missing piece was that I felt like a caged bird. I was missing my freedom. The last straw that led to the putting in of my two-week notice was an upcoming birthday trip for my mother and me.

I asked for and was given permission months before the trip to take the time off. *It must be noted here that I also paid for our flight and hotel arrangements.* Then, there was a change in the management team. The manager who had given me permission was no longer with my team. The company stated I had to go with my current manager's decision. I realized in that moment I had to take my life back. Two weeks later, I was self-employed and on my trip.

I came to realize there was a recurring theme in my life: I had been working so hard to try to keep up appearances, I gave up my freedom. I was, in essence, not living **MY** life. I was living a **LIE**. I was consumed with who I was creating myself to be. I wanted to be the best in all that I did. Instead of being rejected, I wanted to be accepted. In my mind, I thought the only way *that* could happen was if I became a "yes woman" and did all that people asked me to do. I felt like I **had** to become everyone's best friend and put my desires on the back burner to ensure other people had what they wanted. Yes, I was a huge people-pleaser.

Leaving corporate America and becoming a full-time entrepreneur was the catalyst of change in my life. Taking that step allowed me to acknowledge that I am more than my degrees and accomplishments. I am an innovator and a game-changer. I have been an entrepreneur for the last six years. I went from leaving a five-figure salary, going to a zero-figure income, and then recreating five figures in my own business.

The phenomenal thing is that I, along with God, created every dime that has made the five figures in my business. The important thing about telling you that is that if I can do it, you can, too! You can do that thing you thought was impossible.

What is your life telling you your next step is? Do not hesitate or vacillate. Make a move towards the direction your heart is telling you to go. God speaks to your heart. The day I made the decision to become 'just Stevii' was the day I birthed my business and brand *Just Stevii*. The one thing I ran away from most of my life was the one thing that brought me back to life.

During my time as an entrepreneur, God has also blessed me with a mission: to empower, inspire, educate, and motivate women by equipping them with the tools they need to succeed. My greatest belief is this: When women are equipped, there is no stopping their potential. I help them discover, define, and refine their "It Factor". The "It Factor" lets women know who they are and why they are – and helps them stand out in a crowded marketplace while creating more money.

My "It Factor" saved my life. God created it in me before He even created me. Everything in the universe has a purpose. It is important for you to learn what your purpose is so that you can live a life that serves God. You are a solution to someone's problem. If you do not live your life fully, you are blocking someone's blessing. The people who are connected to the watered-down version of you are not meant to be in your life. They are friends with the "false" you. Become the complete version of yourself for the season you are in. We are always in a season of growth and development. The best version of you is the you who is needed for this current time.

My goal is to help every woman who enters my space connect with their "It Factor". When you are confident in your "It Factor", you will be able to boldly speak your truth. Your story may not be rejection. That was mine, and it is one I am still working to overcome daily. As long as you live, you will continue to work through your transparent testimony. I want to encourage you to develop the voice to write and speak yours. Your testimony was not given to you for just you; it was given to you to share and serve others.

I want to congratulate and thank you in advance for having the courage to use your voice and vision as a vessel to change the world. Be excited about your journey!

HERSTORY Reveals His Glory

Growing in Faith
Marlowe Scott © 2015

Our Spiritual Gift of Faith, like the small mustard seed,
Is planted by God and must grow
Into a deep-rooted belief that our Father nurtures
As the sun, winds, and storms of life come and go.

While our fruitful day may not readily come,
God continues the sunshine and rains
And counts each budding leaf one by one.

You see: He knows the end before we do
Because all of His promises are definitely true; and
We must have faith to see the growing-period through.

When we begin to mature and bear the fruit as we should,
We will see the positive outcome of those times we waited
And realize that our God surely has been more than good!

If God is Love, Then Who am I?
"...but rejoices with the truth..."
M.E. Porter

Simply put: I am a liar – or I have been a liar for most of my life. I have the gift of words coupled with the gift of wisdom. Without the Spirit of God working through me, those two gifts are a cocktail for the creation of a profound liar! Now, what I know to be a lie is (**very** simply put) "the intent to deceive". It doesn't matter if the intention is good or if the lie is designed to protect; telling one lie for *any* cause makes you a **LIAR**. That's who I was.

I lied to my mom about having an abortion. I told her I was pregnant, but that the fetus was not viable – and for medical reasons, I could not carry the child. That was such an easy lie to tell because there *was* just a **hint** of truth: I had been considered a high-risk pregnancy case and had experienced several miscarriages (none of which awakened my nothingness).

I lied about my reason for getting married – both times. Yes, I had been somewhat of a professional liar! I married both times to escape the tragedy of having no real life direction and the fear of becoming a welfare case. **That's the truth!**

I lied about my GPA my last semester in college. Lord Jesus...I was struggling so hard, I barely made it out!

There are too many lies to recall, but I know the **biggest** lie I have ever told is one that simply said, "I am good! I am okay. It's fine that he (*choose any he that has ever been in my life – starting with my father*) doesn't love or want me." The truth is I have spent my entire life seeking to be loved and desired by a man.

The greater truth is that I learned to feel nothing instead of allowing that void to be felt. There came a point in my life when I didn't have the capacity to love or be loved.

~~Mistaken~~ by Man, Inspired Through God
Cindy Miller

A true testimony for the *Herstory* project born out of a mere conversation with my Mentor/Coach, Mrs. Marshea Mayfield. I shared with her that the Lord placed it in my spirit to write a book. She then shared with me that she was in the process of writing a book and stated, "...the author is looking for co-authors." I prayed a simple prayer: *If this project is in your will for me, Lord, please let there be some available slots and make provisions for the installment payment.*

At approximately 8:30 p.m., I left home and went to the store. Upon returning, I got a pen and some paper and began to write about me – something I had never done before. I never thought about my story or even realized I had a story. Notice I was writing by FAITH. At 10:05 p.m., a knock came at my back door. To my surprise, my tenant handed me three crisp $100 bills for rent – three days BEFORE the due date! It was more than enough. That was the answer to my prayer, and I immediately knew this was the season to share my story. I've never experienced anything that miraculous and expeditious before!

Let's begin the journey...

My parents (whom I love dearly) conceived me out of wedlock and at a late age in life (my dad has since gone on to be with the Lord). According to the 'world', I was an illegitimate [bastard] child. All of those things qualified me to be a ~~MISTAKE~~. Well, that is not so. Jeremiah said it so profoundly: "*Then the Word of the Lord came to me saying, Before I formed thee in the belly I knew thee; and before I camest forth out of the womb, I sanctified thee and ordained thee a prophet to the nations*" (Jeremiah 1:4-5). The Lord knew me before I came out of my mother's womb, therefore my conception was no surprise to **Him**.

As an infant, I became very ill one night. My eyes began to roll into the back of my head and I had a very high temperature. I was transferred to the hospital by an ambulance. Upon my arrival, the nurse on duty (she was very heavy and plush in size) saw how sick I looked and began running with my stretcher. *Due to her size, she had to turn her body sideways to get through the door.* After a series of examinations, they learned I had a very serious viral infection and needed to be admitted to the hospital for care. However, after finding out my mother did not have insurance, the doctor sent me home to die. My mother nurtured me back to health, and although I was sickly throughout my childhood years, death could not hold me because God had a plan for my life! Praise God! 49 years later and I am **still** here!

As Jeremiah 29:11 (NIV) declares, *"For I know the plans I have for you, declares the Lord; plans to prosper you and not to harm, plans to give you hope and a future."* My life was surrounded by insecurities that shaped how I viewed myself in this world. I always thought I was not supposed to be here and that I was a ~~MISTAKE~~, but God had a plan for my life!

Imagine being a young girl reared in a small city who – daily and shamelessly – viewed herself based on the physicality of having dark skin, puffy eyes, and a space between her front teeth…so often afraid to smile or talk to people because of limited speaking abilities. That young girl was me; very passive, inferior, shy, timid, and having low self-esteem. I was over-compulsive while helping others (a need to be needed), always waiting on someone to validate me while thinking I was not good enough, worthy enough, or even pretty enough. I lived in a world where I was looked down on and often talked to with the expectation to be perfect. I thought I had to be perfect, which is a definite untruth.

Today, as an Ordained Elder, there are some days I still miss the target, feel out of sync, am not in the flow, or simply make ~~MISTAKES~~ and mess up. I am not perfect, but the God I serve is! Somehow, God's love and grace **always** show up…just in time.

HERSTORY Reveals His Glory

I grew to love the Word of God at an early age because it served as a hiding place from the fact that I was a ~~MISTAKE~~. Some of my favorite scriptures were:

"I have shewed you all things, how that so labouring ye ought to support the weak, and to remember the words of the Lord Jesus, how He said, "It is more blessed to give than to receive" (Acts 20:35).

"Beloved, think it not strange concerning the fiery trial which is to try you, as though some strange thing happened unto you: But rejoice, inasmuch as ye are partakers of Christ's sufferings; that, when His glory shall be revealed, ye may be glad also with exceeding joy" (1 Peter 4:12-13).

"But the God of all grace, who hath called us unto His eternal glory by Christ Jesus, after that ye have suffered a while, make you perfect, stablish, strengthen, settle you" (1 Peter 5:10).

"For I reckon that the sufferings of this present time are not worthy to be compared with the glory which shall be revealed in us" (Romans 8:18).

I really believed I had been picked out to be picked on. Nothing came easy to me. I constantly 'went through' things literally all of my life – but God had a greater plan.

Over time, I developed a "back seat mentality". What is a "back seat mentality"? I am glad you asked! It is always getting in the back seat – although the front seat is available. My thought-process was this: *The front seat was not made for me. It was too good for me to sit there. I was a* ~~MISTAKE~~. With those thoughts, I found that I would always allow others to get in the front seat (a.k.a. go before me). This led to me being humble, always in the background or shadowing, and pushing others toward their destinies and visions.

There was one great obstacle I had to overcome. That obstacle was called FEAR: False Evidence Appearing Real. Fear is defined as "a distressing emotion aroused by an impending danger, evil, or pain – whether the threat is real or not". Fear is a basic instinct built in to who we are. My coach says, "Sometimes I have to do it, even if I have to do it scared." Guess what? Even if I messed up, at least I did it!

I contended with the fear of being different and alone. I learned that it really was okay because I was definitely different – but I was never alone.

Matthew 28:18-20 says, *"And Jesus came and spake unto them, saying, "All power is given unto Me in Heaven and in earth. Go ye therefore, and teach all nations, baptizing them in the name of the Father, and of the Son, and of the Holy Ghost: teaching them to observe all things whatsoever I have commanded you: and, lo, I am with you always, even unto the end of the world."* The Lord has always been with me!

As years passed, what I came to realize was the "real" woman was on the inside of me. I grasped the importance of pushing my way through until the "real me" was showing on the outside. The glory of my life's story will help you see that it is only an uncompromising process that leads to the unveiling of God's promises. Yes, I said **process**. It is just that: a process.

I had to remind myself so many times: *Don't fight the process…don't fight the process…don't fight the process!*

Surely, the Lord had a plan for my life. I didn't know the plan and realized I didn't need to know. My outward appearance is my gift wrapping which is subject to be cut, taped, crumpled, torn, ripped, folded, stored to be used again, or even thrown away. The "Real Gift" is on the inside of me. 1 Peter 3:4 (MSG) reads, *"Cultivate inner beauty, the gentle, gracious kind that God delights in."*

I revealed all of my blemishes by talking about each one. For example, as it relates to my dark skin color, I would say, "The blacker the berry, the sweeter the juice!" For my puffy eyes, I would say, "I inherited them from my mom" – and I look like her! For the space between my teeth, I would say, "It is kind of cute!"

The Bible records in Psalm 139:14, *"I will praise thee: for I am fearfully and wonderfully made; marvelous are thy works, and that my soul knoweth right well."* I began to confess what God said about me. Everyone has blemishes – some more noticeable than others. Jesus was the **ultimate** unblemished sacrifice. I had to ask myself the following question: *How was I to get what's inside of me out?* I **had** to find my purpose and walk in it.

As I am writing this, I am opening myself up and being healed! Thank you, Jesus! I thought I was not supposed to be here – but God had a plan for my life.

HERSTORY Reveals His Glory

I started believing the truth. I started believing God's Word. I began to speak out of my mouth what the Word says about me. On a daily basis, my confession is:

I am blessed and not cursed.
I am above and not beneath.
I am the head and not the tail.
I am the righteousness of God.
I am the apple of His eye.
I am the beloved of God.
I am divinely healthy and fully restored.
I am prosperous and walking in a wealthy place.
I am more than a conqueror.
I am accepted in the Beloved.
I am an ambassador for Christ.
I am a Royal Priesthood.
I am a peculiar person.
I am the light of the world.
I am the salt of the earth.
I am reconciled to God.
I am God's workmanship.
I am set free.
I am washed in the Blood.
I am delivered.
I am redeemed.
I am covered under His shadow.
I am free from condemnation.
I am reconciled.
I am healed.
I am loved.
I am chosen.
I am qualified.

I am forgiven.
I am under the shadow of the Almighty.
I am seated with Christ in heavenly places.
I am an overcomer.
I am a recipient of an inheritance.
I am hid in Christ.
I am victorious.
I am a new creature.
I am the elect of God.
I am strong in the Lord.
I am a joint heir with Christ.
I am complete in Him.

My confidence escalated to a new level! My faith catapulted, knowing that *"Faith cometh by hearing and hearing by the Word of God"* (Romans 10:17).

I began to ask myself a laundry list of questions. *What if I became an entrepreneur? What if I became CEO of my own company? What if I write several books? What if I write a bestseller? What if I became a millionaire? What if I became a comedian? What if I became a director, producer, and writer? What if I had lead roles in movies? What if I mentor youth all over the world? What if I became a professional speaker? What if I became a consultant? What if I start a foundation that provides aid to senior citizens? What if I start a summer program for underprivileged youth?*

Inspired by and adapted from the story of *The Little Engine That Could*, I created my own inspirational quote: "I think I can, I think I can, I think I can…I believe I can, I believe I can, I believe I can…I know I can, I know I can, I know can!" According to Philippians 4:13, *"I can do all things through Christ which strengtheneth me."*

Romans 8:28 declares, *"And we know that all things work together for the good to them that love God, to them who are called according to His purpose."* I utilized the former pain of being laughed at and began to make people laugh. The character "Granny" was developed, and my comedy ministry was birthed. *"A merry heart doeth good like a medicine; but a broken spirit drieth bones"* (Proverbs 17:22).

I took my need to help others – along with being gifted to serve – and advanced as an Armorbearer. *"So David came to Saul and stood before him greatly, and he became his Armorbearer"* (1 Samuel 16:21). I took the things that happened in my childhood, and "New Kid on the Block Ministry" came to fruition. *"Train up a child in the way that he should go: and when he is old, he will not depart from it"* (Proverbs 22:6).

An eraser is used to rub something out. ~~MISTAKES~~ can be erased – or marked through. The Lord erased some things in my life; others, He marked through. When I thought I was a ~~MISTAKE~~, all the while, God had a plan for my life. Yes, I am talking about me, but this is really for you.

We can all relate on some level. It is helpful to always remember Jeremiah 29:11 (NIV): *"I know the plans I have for you, plans to prosper you and not harm you, to give you hope and a future."* God has a wonderful plan for your life, so walk in it.

"For the promises of God in him are yea, and in him Amen, unto the glory of God by us" (2 Corinthians 1:20). God used everything I went through for His glory. There was nothing wasted and nothing lost. There were no ~~MISTAKES~~ about it; just the uncompromising process that led me to receive God's promises.

HALLELUJAH!

HERSTORY Reveals His Glory

He Loved Me...In Reverse
Angela Edwards

Back in my "worldly days", you couldn't keep me out of a nightclub on the weekends. I **LIVED** for the weekend when my homegirl (*for the sake of the story, let's name her Yvonne*) and I could hang out until the breaking of a new day – all the while partying until our hearts were content. During that phase of my life, I cannot think of a local (and not-so-distant) club that I didn't grace with my presence. Those were the good, old days...

It was during one of **those** boogie nights that I met 'him'.

You know how when you sometimes see someone, you just **KNOW** you were meant to be in the same place at the same time? You have that moment when you look across the room...and there he is – obviously filled with the same sense of 'knowing' because he's staring not only at, but *through* you. My goodness. The memory of that night brings back a flood of memories that I won't dare entertain here; however, our *chance* meeting – he and I – must be mentioned. It's a significant part of my Herstory. For privacy's sake, we'll just call 'him' Jay.

HERSTORY Reveals His Glory

When Yvonne and I first entered 'Club X', Jay was literally the first man to catch my eye...on that night, anyway. *I was single and free to mingle, so having men catch my eye was a common occurrence.* Our chance-meeting happened on the stairs leading to and from the dance floor. I was heading towards the party, and he was taking a break from it. We locked eyes, gave each other the head nod that silently said, "I see you!" – and then we didn't see each other again for the majority of the night! In that moment, he was just another tall, dark, and handsome man who caught my eye for an instant.

Fast-forwarding to the time the club turned on the lights and told us die-hard party-goers that it was time to go, there he was! He was standing near the exit – staring intently at me. Mr. Handsome beckoned me over, and I was drawn to him like a moth to a flame. I do believe I floated on air over to him because I do not remember my feet making those types of moves. If I knew then like I know now, I would have remained firmly planted alongside Yvonne and ignored the devil in disguise – but I digress. Allow me just a moment to share a bit more about Jay, and you may come to understand why I classified him as such.

When Jay and I formally introduced ourselves, he turned to one of his friends and boldly proclaimed, "This woman right here is going to be my wife one day!" *I had to look around to see who he was referring to! Surely, he was not talking about me – the woman he just shook hands with all of 15 seconds (or less) ago.* As if he read my mind (or perhaps it was the **obvious** look of confusion on my face), he reaffirmed himself by placing his arm around my shoulder, looked me dead in my eyes, and said directly *to* me, "**YOU** are going to be my wife one day." "Umm…Okay" was all I could muster in response. I was blown away by his boldness. I was completely enamored by it, actually.

Alright. Enough about that night. Again, it was imperative to me that you, Dear Reader, understand that the night was extraordinary in every sense of the word. *After all, who literally floats on air in a nightclub?*

Moving along…

Jay and I became an instant 'item'. We connected on **so** many levels. He liked the same types of movies, music, cars, drinks, and **so** much more – and, come to find out, Yvonne and one of **his** friends became involved in a relationship as well! With all of those likenesses, there was no one around who could tell me we weren't meant to fulfill his proclamation that we **WOULD** one day be husband and wife. Life was great! Coming off the heels of a bad marriage and messy divorce some two years earlier, it was nice to be doted over again. Jay fit the bill and filled the role of 'that guy' in my life. He was all that I needed and more…***at that time in my life*** (remember; I was running **WILD** before).

HERSTORY Reveals His Glory

By now, I'm sure you're wondering: *Where did it go wrong?* Well, it went wrong roughly two weeks into our relationship – a relationship that actually lasted **seven years**. *Why so long*, you ask? Simply because I was in love.

To get back to the story…

Roughly two weeks into our relationship, I asked him to run to the store for me to grab a couple of things to make him a special dinner. Running to the store required him using my car to do so. By this time, it wasn't uncommon for him to run an errand or two from time to time. It was never far. A quick trip to the corner store or a drive to pick up a pizza from downtown was the extent of his time behind the wheel of my car. So, when I asked for him to make this run to the store, I never expected to **NOT** see him nor my car for weeks on end.

Police reports were filed – against him and for the missing car. Hospitals both near and far were called. The concern for him grew minute by minute…hour by hour…day by day. His family had no idea where he was (*or so I had been told by the one sister who, I later learned, was a habitual liar who disliked me*). His friends had no idea where he was (*which, I later learned, were a pack full of liars, too*). He simply vanished into thin air! I wondered, "*Had the rapture occurred and I had been left behind?*" I did not understand his sudden disappearance. There was no contact whatsoever to help ease the stress.

Well, here's the truth – in all of its ugliness (a truth I have never shared with anyone until now): When his hateful sister finally decided to tell me the truth of his whereabouts, Jay and my car had been gone for **over** a month. During that time, my life had changed dramatically. I was in constant panic-mode. I was stressed **out**, not eating, not sleeping, losing weight, hair was breaking off, and my other relationships were suffering as well. *Where was my love?*

Jay, Dear Reader, was in a county jail about an hour or so away from my home! Why didn't anyone tell me that simple truth so that I didn't have to go through the changes I did? Simply put: I believe the passage of Scripture that says, *"…your adversary the devil, as a roaring lion, walketh about, seeking whom he may devour…"* (1 Peter 5:8). **After all, how can you have a message for the masses when you're dead and gone – and stress was the killer?**

So as to not bore you with too many minute details, I will quickly explain Jay's tryst to jail. This is as brief as it gets: Jay was a functional crackhead. For those who aren't familiar with the term, a *functional* crackhead is one who will hold down a job, 'take care of home' (as best as the addiction will allow), and, for all intents and purposes, show up in the world as having it all together. I didn't learn that I was involved with that type of individual until I went to visit him in jail with the sole purpose of getting more information on the whereabouts of my car.

The only way he could explain him being a couple of counties away (after a bit of incessant prodding on my part) when he was only supposed to be five minutes away, was to tell me **HIS** whole truth: He was on his way to get high with the money I gave him, got pulled over, and my car was impounded. Why didn't he call? He didn't have my number committed to memory and no one who visited him would give him that information. *Some people are just evil.* Anyway...

All I could say to myself in the moment was, "**NOT AGAIN!**" The 'again' came from the fact that I had divorced a *not-so-functional* crackhead. I had vowed I would be more careful in my choice of mate moving forward. **OOPS!**

Moving the story forward a bit more...

After Jay was released from his 90-day bout in county jail, he wooed me over – again. There I go floating on air...again. What was it about that man that I could not resist? I truly believed there was a decent man hiding within the depths of Jay's soul. I met that man. He was the man I came to love deeply. However, I wasn't prepared to fight the demon that was riding shotgun (the addict).

Our whirlwind of a relationship had more highs than lows. We attended church together – one where his mother was on the pulpit staff. We dated the "old-fashioned way" – meaning we went out to dinner and the movies often (as an example). His friends became my friends (and vice-versa). His sister and I never grew to like each other, but we tolerated each other's presence for Jay's sake. Life was truly good...on most days.

The moral of the story is this, Dear Reader: When people tell you who they are, believe them. I only have myself to blame for the heartache and turmoil I allowed in my life. I could have – **SHOULD HAVE** – walked away the instant "I was on my way to get high" escaped from Jay's lips. I am and remain grateful for God's protection of my *heart*.

For seven years, I gave Jay my heart – in spite of knowing I was fighting a losing battle…again. Addiction is a beast that love alone cannot conquer. Unless individuals have a desire to change their **own** lives for the better, you will be sucked into a world you are not ready to reside in. Scripture tells us to not be unequally-yoked and that righteousness and wickedness have nothing in common (2 Corinthians 6:14). That caution extends beyond the church; it applies to relationships, conversations, and any other form of union known to man.

Believe me when I tell you, Jay's love **was** in reverse. The more I loved, the more he recklessly drove his love backwards and away from me. When I took a stand for myself…when I had enough…I realized God permitted the relationship for a purpose. One day, I was going to tell this story to encourage another. I pray I did God justice.

That is my story – and I wouldn't change a thing.

Abuse is Not Love
Marlowe Scott © 2015

Abuse comes in many forms.
In some cultures and homes,
Abuse is the norm.

It's directed at children and adults, too;
Has abuse ever happened to you?

Have scars – seen and unseen –
Impacted this earthly life?
Have loved-ones inflicted pains, causing deep strife?

What to do? Where to turn for relief?
Will anyone believe my deepening grief?

There has to be a way
To make it through another day.
Help me, Dear Lord; help me, I pray.

I have heard about Jesus
And how He came to save us.
Is Jesus the answer for me?
If so, this is my plea:

Help me, Dear Jesus. Help me right now.
At your throne I throw my cares and humbly bow.
Please relieve the pain; make it go away.
I believe you can, and this I pray.
Thank you for the warm comfort I now feel.
Thank you, Dear Jesus, because I know you can heal.
Take my abuser under your care,
So that no one else will feel the pains I bear.

If God is Love, Then Who am I?
"…love does endure all things…"
M.E. Porter

My journey to love has been **REAL**. I have made great realizations while laying many previous thought-processes to rest. I have had to come clean and lose a few people – but there were those who remained. After all, love does endure all things. But the moment of reconciliation came in the hour that I was no longer permitted to sit in the seat of nothingness. As a mother, delivering from nothingness was perhaps the greatest blessing of my life! To God be the glory for His masterful hand in my love-awakening! Knowing, showing, and receiving love began with an understanding of just how much Jehovah loves us.

I have always heard people say, "God is love", and I believed it…to some degree. I mean, how else could God be described if not 'love'? However, the notion of God being love put me in conflict with **ME**. If God was love, then who was I? Hatred? Can you see how that would create a major inward-conflict? I lived quite a few years of my teenage and adult life seeing myself as "hate" because I did not truly know or understand love.

Aha! Moment:
Intellect, reason, and lies are not friends of LOVE.

"Then He said, "I tell you the truth; unless you turn from your sins and become like little children, you will never get into the Kingdom of Heaven" (Matthew 18:3 (NLT)).

I truly understand that passage of scripture today. Children have the gift of loving unconditionally – void of reason and intellect – and do not come with lies planted in their hearts. Turning from sin, relinquishing pride, living in truth, serving others, and believing in self all require a childlike belief in the power of God's love for us.

If God is love, then who am I?

I am His own workmanship (Ephesians 2:10).

I am the apple of His eye (Psalm 17:8).

I am the righteousness of God (2 Corinthians 5:21).

I am fearfully and wonderfully created (Psalm 149:14).

I am more than a conqueror (Romans 8:31).

If God is love, then who am I? I am LOVE because I am created in His own image (Genesis 1:27).

To God be the glory forever and ever.

HERSTORY Reveals His Glory

In closing...

The HERSTORY project was brought to life in October 2013. It was part of the Thursday night ministry call for Motivationally ME. Not long after the ministry was started – as a Facebook page and FreeConferenceCall.com phone number – it was laid on my heart to create a platform for women to share their testimonies with other women as a source of healing.

I remember our very first guest. I was a little nervous to invite her to speak because I felt as though the ministry was not established enough for someone who seemed to be already on her way to come share with us. Boy, was I wrong! Ms. Cheron K. Griffin responded to my request almost immediately. Her response was so powerful **to** and **for** me: "Yes! Of course! I am honored and humbled that you would seek me out to share with your group of ladies!" I am not sure I ever communicated this to anyone, but her words gave life to my vision; they confirmed that I was, indeed, in the right space, doing the right thing at the right time.

Since then, we have heard some extraordinary stories of triumph and redemption: domestic violence, recovery from drugs and alcohol, serial infidelity, hidden homosexuality, giving birth to be loved, and struggling just to be loved at all costs. **BUT GOD!**

From time to time, I go back and listen to the replays of the stories that were told – just to remind me how far God has brought us from. I am forever grateful for the power of the testimony...the story: ***HERSTORY***.

HERSTORY Reveals His Glory

As we make the leap into putting pen to paper and allowing the world – not just a few ladies on a phone call – to share in the power of our stories, the prayer is very simple:

Father God, in the name of your Son, Jesus; let the stories shine light in dark places. Heal those who are broken. Revive where there has been death. Let us all overcome by the power of ***HERSTORY***! **Amen**.

The Tellers of "HERSTORY"

HERSTORY Reveals His Glory

MY STORY...

HERSTORY Reveals His Glory

HERSTORY Reveals His Glory

HERSTORY Reveals His Glory

HERSTORY Reveals His Glory

HERSTORY Reveals His Glory

HERSTORY Reveals His Glory

HERSTORY Reveals His Glory

HERSTORY Reveals His Glory

HERSTORY Reveals His Glory

HERSTORY Reveals His Glory

HERSTORY Reveals His Glory

HERSTORY Reveals His Glory

HERSTORY Reveals His Glory

HERSTORY Reveals His Glory

HERSTORY Reveals His Glory

HERSTORY Reveals His Glory

Authors' Bios

Tiffany Campbell

To God be the glory: It is because of You that I am here unapologetically telling my story. God, thank you for the strength to get over those hills I have climbed and those to come. My 'HERSTORY' is dedicated to my family – in particular my aunts who took me into their home and offered their love and support during some of the hardest moments in my life. I thank you for being patient and understanding – even when I was trying to shut you out. The grief I felt at those times was heavy and dark. Believe me when I say: Your efforts were recognized. To my friends who never once judged me and stayed true, I love you. I would like to thank my husband for teaching me what love truly is; you helped me grow into the woman I am today, accepting all of my flaws and never giving up on me. To my in-laws: God knew that I needed you in my life. Thank you. Finally, to Marilyn Porter: My gratitude to you is overwhelming. Thank you for granting me this platform to tell my story. This has given me healing in ways I never could have imagined. Love you all…

Angela Edwards

Angela is CEO of Pearly Gates Publishing LLC. Through her ministry, she works closely alongside both new and seasoned authors who have messages that empower, inspire, and educate their respective audiences. Birthed in February 2015, Angela's publishing house has produced numerous best sellers, with some claiming the coveted #1 spot. She says, "Operating with transparency and integrity keeps me in line with God's mission for Pearly Gates Publishing." She is happily married to James Edwards and resides in Houston, TX.

Gail Freeman

After a lifelong battle of drug addiction and abuse, Gail overcame all odds and is now living a productive life through the grace of God. Founder and CEO of *Just Us Girls Camden County – A NJ Nonprofit Corporation*, she now gives back and empowers others to find their strength to overcome and live a life of productivity. A portion of her life's story is presently featured in the Best-Selling anthology, *God Says I am Battle-Scar Free: Testimonies of Abuse Survivors*. Gail's story will also be shared in several other forthcoming books, including her own autobiography. Gail actively labors to raise funds for her organization, which services the homeless and senior communities. She has been recognized for her service by the City Council of Camden, New Jersey and the Camden Metro Police Department.

Famira M. Green

Famira is The Diamond DIVA! She's known as Your Visual IMPACTologist™. She's Chief Visionary Officer of Diamond DIVA International. She shows women Speakers, Coaches, and Social Change Agents how to create show-stopping brands that change the world. As a Visual Branding Master and an Image Style Guru, she helps her clients brand themselves and create masterful impact in their industry. Famira is also an International Best-Selling Author, Speaker, and Thought Alchemist.

Cindy Miller

Cindy is known as having a "Servant's Heart" and firmly believes in helping others. She is an Ordained Elder and currently serves as Pastoral Assistance, Administrator, and Youth Director at I am Covered Ministries under the leadership of Dr. Cynthia Plummer and Overseer Jenette B. Stokes. She is the Founder/CEO of New Kid on the Block Ministry, an outreach ministry that helps youth discover, develop, and display their God-given gifts. Also known as "Comedian Granny", Cindy writes, produces, and directs Gospel stage plays. Born in Waynesboro, MS, she is the youngest of four siblings.

Stevii Mills

Stevii specializes in creating concepts, leadership development, business mentorship, and networking. With a Bachelor of Arts Degree in Public Relations and a Master's of Science Degree in Human Resources, she is able to align and execute visions, concepts, products, events, and speaking engagements for women who are dedicated to using their network marketing opportunity as a platform to brand themselves and launch their dreams. Stevii's primary goal is empowering women to tap into their God-give "It Factor". When you connect with Stevii, you are guaranteed to have fun, learn, and grow!

Adrienne Santana

Happily married, Adrienne and her husband share three wonderful children and two grandchildren. She first gives all credit and honor to God for the life He has gifted her with. While a mother herself, she attended Franklin Pierce College. It was there she was able to nurture her love for the written word. As Founder of "Legacy of the Lotus Fund", Adrienne teaches women and young adults to write their own legacy and gives them a platform as a published author.

Marlowe Scott

Marlowe is committed to using her God-given talents to witness and bless others. As one of Pearly Gates Publishing LLC's Best-Selling authors, her inspired poetry enriches both of her published works: *Spiritual Growth: From Milk to Strong Meat* and *Believing Without Seeing: The Power of Faith*. Marlowe's business, M.R.S. Inspirations, provides hand-crafted designs to give love and comfort to recipients.

Christina "Chris Dannie" Wilson

Christina is a young woman on the rise – 18 years young, to be exact. She is an aspiring actress and a profound writer of poetry and lyrics. Chris has recorded a CD featuring her spoken word and has a dream of someday preaching the Word of God in her own unique way. She is the first-born child of Christopher Wilson and the middle child in the Porter-Wilson trio. Chris is a Performing Arts major at Alabama State University and is also pursuing a degree in Special Education. Her ultimate goal in life is to open a nonprofit organization that will service children with learning difficulties – especially Austim – by teaching them through the arts. Chris Dannie is also a talented songstress and loves to worship the Lord in song.

HERSTORY Reveals His Glory

HERSTORY Authors' Favorite Quotes

M.E. Porter: *"When all is well with my soul, then all I well in the world."*

Adrienne Santana: *"Let patience have her perfect work."* (James 1:4)

Angela Edwards: *"Integrity is everything."*

Famira Green: *"Comparison is an act of violence against the self."* ~ Iyanla Vanzant

Stevii Mills: *"To whom much is given, much is required."* (Luke 12:48)

Gail Freeman: *"A day clean is a day won."*

Christina Wilson: *"You only live once."*

Marlowe Scott: *"…seek ye first the kingdom of God, and His righteousness…"* (Matthew 6:33)

Cindy Miller: *"Opportunity knocked this morning, and I opened the door."*

HERSTORY Reveals His Glory

M.E. Porter's Bio

M.E. Porter is well-respected and admired in many circles for her passionate techniques that drive others to reach their full potential. Born in a poverty-stricken, drug-infested neighborhood of southern New Jersey, even as a child she and those around her knew that she would break free of poverty's limitations and somehow achieve excellence.

Excellence is achieved in dedicated service to those whom she is called to serve.

She is a woman who wears many hats; mother of three beautiful daughters, minister, motivator, mentor, and teacher. She is a professional Life Coach and speaker, but most importantly, she is a woman unashamed to walk in her spiritually-infused gifts. It is those very gifts that make her a highly sought-out writer, speaker, and spiritual advisor. In an arena of big, bold promises, M.E. makes only one: "I will always speak to your soul."

A graduate of The University of Maryland, this woman of God is equipped to serve her clients and audiences with a wealth of academic knowledge, which accompanies her life experience, wisdom, and spiritual grounding. Having endured two divorces, several miscarriages, childhood rape, the rejection of her natural father, and many other abuses in her life, she stands to serve the world as a soul-healer – having learned for herself that if your soul is broken, the very foundation to every other possibility is jeopardized.

M.E. is the CEO of M.E. Unlimited, LLC – The ME Brand, which is a Christian personal development, coaching, and healing organization. Here, she avails herself to all of those to whom she is called.

M.E. is also a cast member on the upcoming reality television show, "The Successors", and a Best-Selling author four times over. She is most proud of her book "The Pieces of ME (And You)".

Her mantra is simply: Speak. Pray. Love.

www.marilyneporter.com
FB /IAmMEPorter
Twitter @SoulutionSage

HERSTORY Reveals His Glory

THERE IS HEALING IN TELLING THE STORY

HERSTORY Reveals His Glory

HERSTORY book 2 will be released in December 2016. If you would like to be a part of the vision, please contact:

M.E. Porter

info@marilyneporter.com

404-500-8722

HERSTORY Reveals His Glory

HERSTORY Reveals His Glory

www.ingramcontent.com/pod-product-compliance
Lightning Source LLC
Chambersburg PA
CBHW071518080526
44588CB00011B/1470